CW00595111

Living Japan

Essays on Everyday Life in Contemporary Society

Edited by
Harumi Kimura

Translated by
Haruko Miyazaki
Yuriko Takahashi
and Others

GLOBAL
ORIENTAL

LIVING JAPAN
ESSAYS IN EVERYDAY LIFE IN CONTEMPORARY SOCIETY
Edited by Harumi Kimura
Translated by H. Miyazaki, Y. Takahashi and Others

First published in 2009 by
GLOBAL ORIENTAL LTD
PO Box 219
Folkestone
Kent CT20 2WP
UK

www.globaloriental.co.uk

© Global Oriental Ltd 2009

ISBN 978-1-905246-86-1

All rights reserved. No part of this publication
may be reproduced or transmitted in any form or by any
electronic, mechanical or other means, now known
or hereafter invented, including photocopying and
recording, or in any information storage or retrieval
system, without prior permission in writing from
the publishers.

British Library Cataloguing in Publication Data
A CIP catalogue entry for this book is available
from the British Library Athonoevn Prees, Gateshead, Tyne and wear

Set in Garamond 11.5 on 13pt by IDSUK (DataConnection) Ltd
Printed and bound in England by Athenaeum Press, Gateshead, Tyne and Wear

Contents

****

Foreword

Harumi Kimura

****

As the title suggests, the essays in this book deal with the everyday lives of ordinary Japanese people.

These days, all countries throughout the world are closely linked with one another. No country is independent of the others, in high technology as well as in politics and the economy. Every nation is far more influenced by other nations than ever before, and has come to have far greater and broader exchanges with the others – in culture, art and literature. The number of people from around the world travelling abroad has increased remarkably.

Japan produced *The Tale of Genji*, the oldest novel in the world. Animated cartoons, Japan's leading art form (*Animé*), have attracted global attention. The everyday life of the ordinary Japanese people, on the other hand, remains hardly known to the rest of the world. I have come to this point of view based on my personal experience. Thirty years ago, I stayed in London, accompanying my husband, a psychologist, sent to England by the Ministry of Education in Japan. Great Britain has been an advanced country and admired most by the Japanese as a model of Western civilization since Japan abandoned its isolation policy in the middle of the nineteenth century and began to import Western culture and institutions. Moreover, I had specialized in English literature at university and had plenty of access to England. I was convinced that I had a wider knowledge and understanding of the state of affairs there, as well as English literature and history, than most Japanese did.

After living in London as a housewife, however, I found that all the information about England available in Japan was entirely lacking any insights into the lives of ordinary people – for example, how they sell meat at a butcher's, how they smile at passers-by when the eyes meet, how they are fond of gardening.

I wrote essays about these surprising discoveries and they were published in a book entitled *Letters from London at Twilight.* The book soon won popularity and immediately became a best-seller, because those aspects of the English way of life which were unknown to the Japanese were introduced by a Japanese woman who provided a window into the everyday lives of ordinary people. The popularity of the book may have been a pointer as to how many Japanese are interested in England. The book was awarded the eighth Ohya-Soichi Non-fiction Prize – the most prestigious non-fiction prize in Japan.

Now, thirty years later – here I am editing a book which contains essays introducing the everyday life of contemporary Japanese society. The essays have been translated into English so that they can be read by people in the United Kingdom and the United States, as well as other English-speaking countries around the world. I hope the book will give the reader a genuine insight into today's 'living Japan'.

During the past thirty years, as we all know, the world situation has been gradually changing and it has become more and more necessary for the people of each country to let the other nations know about the particular value systems that inform their way of life, their feelings and their thoughts. Japan, with its very advanced high technology, is a major Asian power and was the most Westernized in its earliest stages of industrialization; and yet it retains its own particular approach to life and the way it conducts itself, which you will discover in this book. The Japanese ethos is well integrated with nature and quite different from that of Judao-Christian cultures.

Is it really an exaggeration to say that the Japanese perception of worth and value has been attracting the attention of the world in the twenty-first century?

A number of research institutions around the world, especially those in universities, have been putting increasing emphasis on the study of Japan. In this context, the publication of *Living Japan* is of great significance, because it reveals a variety of common feelings which are rarely recognized in international relationships. Some contributions to this book may present the foreign reader with great difficulty in understanding what might be perceived as very alien ways of life. But that only reinforces one of the main purposes of this volume: to promote an understanding of each other across the boundaries of culture, which is sure to lead to greater stability and world peace in the future.

Twenty years ago, I established an organization known as KEG, which stands for Kimura-Harumi Essayist Group. It consists of about fifty members whose ages range from their forties to their eighties. They have all taught how to write essays as lecturers at lifelong education classes or have written essays for various media. What they have devoted themselves to most, however, is the pleasure of writing essays themselves, sometimes to record their life, other times to write their own history, or simply as a means of self-expression. Most of the essays contained in this book were written by KEG members.

Their essays were not written especially for the book. Consequently, they do not represent a systematic or exhaustive introduction and explanation of Japanese life and culture. For example, Mt Fuji is mentioned in some pieces as the highest, world-famous mountain in Japan, but it is not written about as a way of explaining the Japanese mentality. It is the mere sight of Mt Fuji which often happens to catch the writer's attention in her or his everyday life. This daily scene adds to the reality of the relationship between the mountain and Japanese everyday life.

In selecting the essays to be included in this book, I had to exclude some whose theme seemed too difficult to translate into English. In such cases, I felt there was a certain limit to intercultural communication of our daily life and customs. Even so, I did my best to introduce as many examples of Japanese traditional culture, events, life-experiences and human relationships as possible.

Of course, through this book, I should like you the reader to gain some understanding of Japanese culture. But at the same time, I hope that you will also enjoy reading the essays as literary works in their own right. After all, this is what the authors set out to achieve in the first place.

All the essays were originally written in Japanese. Some of the writers translated their works themselves, but most of the essays were rendered into English by the translators best qualified to do so; each of them is introduced at the end of the volume.

PART 1

AT THE FOOT OF MOUNT FUJI

1.

At the Foot of Mt Fuji

Aiko Hamada

****

'Let's go and see Mt Fuji tomorrow!' My younger daughter, who was looking at the weather forecast, suddenly said. It was just after dinner on Friday, 20 February last year.

'We never get good weather like this in February,' her sister chimed in.

'That's true!' I agreed in spite of myself. Our family trips have always been like this ever since the girls were children. Whenever he could find the time for a holiday, my husband would take to the wheel and drive us somewhere as if acting on the proverb, 'Make haste to do good'. Even now when there are only the three of us, my daughters and I have not outgrown that habit. The girls immediately began to discuss where to go.

'How about Lake Kawaguchi? A hotel where we can see Mt Fuji.' My words decided the destination. My older daughter phoned a hotel and reserved our rooms. 'We're leaving at ten o'clock,' she reminded her sister, who is a late riser.

When I woke up at eight o'clock the next morning, the late riser was already having breakfast. 'Mummy, hurry up. I'll go to the garage, get the car washed and fill it up.'

Her sister was getting ready, too. Well, well! I decided to prepare a picnic lunch for all of us.

We left right on schedule, the younger one at the wheel. We joined the Tomei Expressway at the Yokohama Aoba junction and continued our pleasant drive.

'Mummy, would you like to drive?' We changed places at the service area and I took the wheel. I hadn't driven on an expressway for a while and it was quite stimulating. We were fast approaching Mt Fuji.

On leaving the expressway at Gotemba interchange, I handed back the wheel to my daughter. I find driving on a winding road a little difficult now that I am over sixty. My other daughter, who doesn't drive, concentrated on serving tea to whoever was driving.

We reached Lake Kawaguchi at about noon. Mt Fuji in all its snow-capped dignity was standing tall against the winter sky. The temperature was 15 degrees Celsius. There was no wind and the sun was warm. We spread out our picnic lunch on the grass by the lake.

'Daddy liked to eat lunch like this, too, didn't he? We were always together, the four of us . . .' It was my older daughter who started to speak. My husband always used to be with us and watched over us in his gentle way. It is already sixteen years since he suddenly passed away but the precious memories I have stored away carefully at the bottom of my heart return all the more vividly in my happy moments.

We drove around the lake once and then checked in at the hotel. Up till now we had always shared one room, but I had decided that I should not depend so much on my children and start to become more independent, so this time I had reserved a Japanese-style room for myself next to my daughters' room. We soaked ourselves in the hot spring bath together and then retired to our rooms until it was time for dinner. But my daughters kept popping into my room in turn asking, 'Aren't you lonely?' Each time I answered, 'I'm fine' and eventually they stopped coming in. Well, that's OK. It was much quieter and more peaceful like this. And anyway I really can't keep up with the topics or the pace of their conversation. I enumerated reasons why I was stoically keeping my own company. I lay down on the tatami floor, looked up at the wooden ceiling and counted the knots. I couldn't help thinking, 'If only my husband were beside me . . .' I pulled myself together again and walked out onto the balcony. Mt Fuji was soaring right in front of me. How beautiful it was to see the mountain surface covered with snow, glowing red in the evening sun. 'How beautiful this is! Thank you, dear,' I said to my husband, quietly feeling his presence. Then, all of a sudden, the two girls came bursting into my room shouting, 'Mummy, are you watching this?' How noisy these girls are! But all the same I was happy to look at the mountain as we chatted, the three of us together standing side by side.

After dinner, we went for a walk. Candles representing the height of Mt Fuji, 3776 of them, were lit all along the lake, and the faint, flickering lights of the candles reflecting on the surface of the water created a magical scene. They were celebrating the night before the eve of 23 February, Mt Fuji Day, and there were going to be fireworks for thirty minutes from eight o'clock. Unlike the fireworks of the summer festival, few people were around and it was altogether a quieter affair. I strolled along shoulder-to-shoulder with my daughters, looking at the few stalls that were open. Then we heard an announcement that the fireworks were starting. We sat on a bench by the shore to watch large and small fireworks go off in the middle of the lake with a big booming noise. The fireworks spread out in the clear starry sky of winter, showering down on us and disappearing into the bottom of the lake. The fleeting magnificence of this spectacular sight moved me deeply. We rejoiced over this unexpectedly wonderful experience although it had lasted only a short while and went back to the hotel.

The next morning, I woke up before six o'clock. Maybe because of the hot spring bath, I had a very good night's sleep and woke up feeling refreshed. I opened the sliding *shoji* door and caught my breath. I hurried out onto the balcony. The sun was just about to rise. The white snow-clad surface of the mountain was gradually turning orange, glowing in the sun. It was as if a brocade kimono sash were being woven little by little. I found myself joining my hands in prayer at the sight of the awesome presence of the mountain.

'You didn't see Mt Fuji glowing in the morning sun, did you?' I bragged to my daughters at breakfast. They said they were talking until early in the morning. When I said that they must have been talking about something trivial anyway, they replied with a straight face, 'No, we were seriously discussing our future plans.' Although past their mid-thirties, they often seem to be bickering over trifles at home, so it was good for them to sleep side by side on a trip, just the two of them. I made a silent wish for them to continue to be on good terms throughout their lives.

On our way back, we decided to drive to the fifth station of Mt Fuji. When we entered the gate of the Fuji Spiral Line, the temperature was 15.5 degrees. The sun was shining warmly and it was hard to believe it was still winter, but snow removed from the road was piled up high and firm on both sides of the road. We passed the first station and then the second.

'The temperature outside is eight degrees right now. Oh, it's already five. Wow, it's only one degree! I wish my weight would go down this fast.'

'So do I.'

From the back seat, I anxiously warned my daughter to drive carefully, as she joked with her sister. The wind blew against the windscreen. Powdery snow was fluttering around. As we had feared, all traffic was stopped at the fourth station. Not many cars were in the parking area. Shivering from the cold, we took photos standing in front of the 2020 metres signboard to show we had been there.

When we made our way down, we found that the weather was fine at the foot of the mountain. We looked back and saw the white cap of Mt Fuji peeking through the clouds.

'Nothing can beat Mt Fuji. It's the greatest mountain in Japan, isn't it?' The girls looked at each other and seemed deeply moved. I, too, looked up at the mountain, thankful that I was able to stand there in good health together with my two daughters.

TRANSLATED BY H. MIYAZAKI AND Y. TAKAHASHI

2.

Cherry Blossoms Cannot Be Replaced

Kyoko Okuda

****

We enjoy seeing plenty of examples of cherry blossoms on television during the season when they are in full bloom. The sight of them makes me want to go out to see them for myself.

This year, I decided to go cherry-blossom viewing at Hirosaki and Kakunodate in the northeastern part of Japan during the consecutive holidays that take place at the beginning of May. I went there with my husband; the journey took three hours by the super express train.

On arriving at Hirosaki Park, I found the moat lined with cherry trees stretching far away. Every tree seemed strong and splendid; the blossoms in bloom stretched over the moat and looked lovely even when viewed across the moat.

'There's more cherry blossom here than anything I have ever seen,' I said.

'You are right,' answered my husband. He appeared to be struck with admiration and awe at such a beautiful sight.

Once in the park, I had another surprise. Every tree's branches were fully extended, at the top of which pink blossoms were in full bloom. There were about thirty thousand tourists there. Many of them were having lunch on their own mats, but the park was so large that it did not look messy despite the large number of visitors. One type of tree known as Somei Yoshino, the most popular kind of cherry tree, is a hundred and twenty years old, the oldest in Japan. The usual life-span of a cherry tree is fifty or sixty years, yet this ancient one has as many blossoms in bloom as any of the younger ones. As far as I was concerned, I was convinced that Hirosaki should be designated the most picturesque site for cherry blossoms in Japan.

The cherry trees in the park were originally donated by the citizens of Hirosaki about a century ago, towards the end of the Meiji Period, and now number more than 2,600. In those days the people were generally so poor that all their efforts went into supporting themselves.

'Why did they choose to plant cherry trees which do not bear edible fruit?' enquired my husband.

'The people living here are confined indoors in the snow all through the long winter, and look forward to renewing their hope in the future in spring when they see the cherry blossoms in bloom. I presume that's the reason,' I said and reflected on many other things.

In Kakunodate, the cherry blossoms were also in full bloom, forming a blossom tunnel extending for two thousand metres along the banks of the Ekinai-gawa river. The local inhabitants were enjoying a meal on their own mats. The sight was quite splendid and they looked so happy.

Traditional agriculture was labour-intensive. Farm workers were kept very busy and were always short-handed. Naturally local inhabitants must have got together and helped one another. They must have tried to establish better mutual understanding over a meal before they set to work.

Cherry blossoms come into full bloom all at once and fall in a week. The Japanese feel that there is something gallant and admirable in that process. Each petal is rather small, but the petals in one tree as a whole create a splendid sight. We get excited in early spring when the climate becomes milder, anticipating our enjoyment of the cherry blossoms. No other flower or blossom is loved so much by the Japanese as cherry blossoms which make them so happy. I admire the wisdom of our Japanese forefathers who introduced cherry blossoms to Japanese life. I say to myself, 'Cherry blossoms can never be replaced by anything else!'

After the cherry blossoms fall, the moats I visited this year will be covered with fallen petals and present another wonderful view. I should like to revisit those places.

TRANSLATED BY N. KUMABE

3.

The Most Popular Cherry Tree Variety in Japan: A Hit Commodity

Kunio Machida

****

This year, as usual, the cherry blossom season has passed in the twinkling of an eye. Earlier this year I made up my mind to enjoy to my heart's content the blossoming of the cherry trees from beginning to end. As early as in the first week of March, I began to take a regular close look at the cherry trees which stood in an impressive row in the park near my house. In the middle of the month, however, the bare branches still looked dead as if it were still mid-winter. There was no sign whatsoever that they would bloom. Then, in the last week of the month, a number of small lumps like buds appeared on the top of the branches. The tops of the lumps became green. In a few days they turned pink, and I knew that they were blossom buds. A week later they started to open.

Without doubt the blossoms were at their best during their first week. The pink-tinged white blossoms made a beautiful contrast to the dark brown tree trunk. Their beauty was short-lived, however. By the middle of April, the blossoms were past their peak. Some of them were left on the branches, but the beautiful colour contrast between the blossoms and the trunk, disappeared, as green leaves came out, and finally the blossoms themselves rapidly lost their beauty. The period between the opening and the peak of the blooming was no more than two weeks. In such a short time the drama, which can only be performed once a year, was over.

From March into April the cherry blossom front rapidly heads north along Japan's extended archipelago. In each district the blossoming period is very brief. During this time, however, the mountains, fields and towns are all painted in pink-tinged white. The strongest appeal of cherry blossoms lies in their togetherness. Each blossom is rather small, but, when a single tree, a row of trees and a large group of trees bloom all together, the blossoms become the most beautiful. When they are linked together and stretch like clouds or mist, we feel as if we have been magically transported into a dream world.

One day, I was surprised to find that a small tree in a corner of the garden, which I had not noticed before, was in fact a cherry tree, because it produced pinkish white blossoms all at the same time. Since it was usually ignored I imagined it wanting to assert itself once a year, just as modest people want to assert themselves sometimes.

I hear that foreign visitors to Tokyo this year were much impressed with the cherry blossoms. Boarding a coach they went from the airport to a hotel in the centre of the city. The coach drove along the Metropolitan Expressway, left the tunnel and at Chidorigafuchi passed beneath the canopy of cherry blossoms at their best. 'How, fantastic!' they exclaimed with one voice, expressing their admiration at the amazing sight. They could not contain their excitement for some time. It was the warmest welcome offered by this country. They were the luckiest visitors, indeed.

It is true, a lot of people in the world love flowers and blossoms. People in Europe maintain seasonal flowers along the streets and on window sills all year round, while we Japanese concentrate only on the cherry blossoms during the brief time in spring and, when they are gone, wait for them to come again the next year, without paying any particular attention to other flowers. Perhaps it is part of our national character only to enjoy the best flower at one particular time.

However, what I have just said is not true of all cherry trees in Japan. The truth is that I have only referred to one popular variety, that is, the Somei Yoshino variety. The old saying, 'Blossoms are short-lived' is particularly true of this variety. The blooming date of cherry trees forecast by TV is that of the Somei Yoshino kind. It is true that the Somei Yoshino variety is very typical, but there are other kinds of cherry trees, which come into bloom at different times. For example, the Kawazu-sakura variety starts to bloom in February. The blossoms of the Sato-zakura variety last until May. The fact is that the Somei Yoshino variety accounts for sixty to seventy per cent of all cherry trees in Japan.

These percentages remind me of the business world. It is very difficult for one commodity to reach sixty to seventy per cent market share. The Somei Yoshino was first produced about 150 years ago. What is the secret of the high percentage reached by this variety despite its fairly short history? I read books in the library and learned about the production of the new variety. Towards the end of the Tokugawa Period (around 1860) a horticulturalist (whose name is unknown), who lived in Somei, Edo (the old name of Tokyo), produced and began to sell a hybrid of the Ooshima-zakura and Edo-Higan varieties. The former was characterized by its a large petals and the latter by blossoming before the leaves were out. The new variety could not be grown from seed, since one variety had to be grafted to the other. However, grafting was fairly easy, so the new variety spread rapidly across the country. The Somei Yoshino trees propagated by grafting might as well be a clone from a single tree, so they bloomed almost at the same time.

Before the Second World War, when the Japanese made parks and built Shinto shrines in China and Manchuria, they always planted cherry trees. Japanese nationalism, therefore, helped the spread of cherry trees far and wide. The Somei Yoshino was a variety which could be quickly produced to meet demand.

It has the following qualities: 1. The trees bloom before the leaves come out. 2. The blossoms come out almost at the same time. 3. They bear no fruit, but the blossoms are beautiful. 4. It is easy to mass-produce them. Such qualities have satisfied Japanese needs. For this reason the new variety has spread rapidly across the country and has become the typical cherry tree in Japan.

The production of the Somei Yoshino cherry tree can be compared to the development of cameras and televisions. Japanese ingenuity, which is now displayed in the high-tech industry of this country, was revealed by an obscure horticulturist as far back as 150 years ago.

I wonder what the horticulturalist was like and how he was rewarded for the production of such a successful new variety; of course, if he were living today he would be certainly honoured by the president of the company for developing a hit commodity.

TRANSLATED BY S. KURAMOCHI

4.

The Mountains Are Living

Mikiko Tsunoda

****

The first sunrise of the year

With countless stars twinkling and the moon also shining in the clear sky above the tops of the cedars, I do not need to use my torch to light the way ahead. It is so bright. Climbing higher, we find yesterday's snow piled a foot deep and frozen hard among the leafless trees. With the branches casting their clear-cut shadows on the snowy trail, I feel as if I am stumbling over the branches themselves. The moonlight is so bright. The eastern sky is now faintly grey. Half an hour and the sun rises. We must hurry up.

'Here we are. We've made it!'

We are now at the summit of Mt Yakuradake, 2,800 feet high, which has taken two-and-a-half hours to walk up.

Nobody else is here on the wide, flat top, which is covered with snow. In the twilight sky we can clearly see the Hakone mountains in the foreground and Mt Fuji with a gently sloping foot to the south-west. Edwin, my fellow climber, points his finger.

'Look! The sun is rising over there!'

The red shining sun rises as if protruding from the orange-coloured horizon of Sagami Bay on our left. In a twinkling the snow-covered top of Mt Fuji becomes pink-coloured. It is a breathtaking scene. It is more spectacular than I had expected.

How happy we are to view the first sunrise of the year from the top of the mountain!

With fingers stiff with cold I take some pictures. We set up a tent and rest inside. I take out a portable gas-cylinder.

It is almost too cold for the gas to burn strongly. It takes a long time to boil water. At last we pour the hot water into a cup of dried noodles for breakfast.

Every time I climbed this mountain in the past, I wanted to view the first sunrise of the year from its summit and asked some friends of mine to join me, but without success. At last Edwin, a mountain-loving student from abroad, said yes.

I am grateful to him for getting up as early as 2 a.m. on the morning of the first day of the year and accompanying his mountaineering-crazy host mother.

Mt Megamiyama with the remaining snow

It is now May, but in the Tohoku provinces, the northern district of Japan, it is still early spring. Mt Megamiyama stands hazy in the intermittent rain falling. It is fresh with the new-born leaves of beech trees. I notice the barks of trees which are smooth and characteristically speckled.

This is a mountain among the Ou Mountain Range, located in the county border between Akita-ken and Iwate-ken. About 3,300 feet high, it has a primeval pure beech forest. As we, two friends and I, climb higher, I find the trail covered with the remaining snow and the new-born leaves sparse on the tree-tops. It makes me realize we are now fairly high up. There is complete silence except that we sometimes hear birds chirping. My friends also walk up in silence. Although we do not say a word to each other, we know we are very happy now that we are cradled in the mountain air.

I stumble on countless baby beech trees at my feet. I kneel down and touch one of them. Two round leaves, which have sprung from a cupule, face each other. These new-born trees have already taken root in the humus soil, which is composed of fallen leaves. I have never seen baby beech trees, although I have been climbing mountains for many years.

Around us we find trees as young as two or three years. Above us big trees as old as two hundred years spread their branches majestically like patron-gods of the forest. The primeval forest of beech trees, which are the source of life, nature's water reservoir, reminds me of the important role it has been playing from time immemorial.

By the way, the beech forest in the Tanzawa mountains, located near Tokyo, the megalopolis, stands in sharp contrast to this forest. There the beech forest floor is covered with bamboo bushes, because of acid mist and lack of water. The trees cannot naturally regenerate themselves. Even if a cupule falls, it will be impossible for a baby tree to take root. Besides, some beech trees are dying.

Here in the primeval forest of beech trees, I stand up, my heart filling with pleasure, and take a deep breath. I smell the soothing smell of the mountain. I feel the mountain air softly touching my skin. Rain drops are falling noiselessly. The green rain drops into my eyes. I am in absolute bliss.

God's White Mountains

I wonder why it is so bright.

I hold my breath for a moment when I come out of the tent at midnight. It is not as bright as in the daytime, true, but I can clearly see small stones at my feet.

The full moon in the cloudless sky throws such a bright and cool light. Big stars in the sky are twinkling in yellow, blue and white.

In the foreground I see peaks of the Karakoram Himalayas as high as 23,000 feet and as jagged as a saw's teeth. They are Urdkas Peak, Rakaposhi Peak and Hisper Peak. I can even clearly see mountain folds, which look near enough to touch.

Against the crystal-clear and cobalt-blue sky the snow-covered tops look as if they are floating in mid-air, while the mountain foot is of a dark colour, as if drawn in Chinese ink. What an incredible sight! Why does it look so? Is it because the air is thin? We are now staying at the camp as high as 13,000 feet. There are neither trees nor grass on the surface. The snow- and ice-covered tops reflect back all light. I have never heard of nor seen such majestic and grand scenery – even in pictures.

It is so bright.

However, the brightness has not a bit of warmth in it. It denies all life, freezes everything and absorbs any sound, leaving only stillness to us.

This is God's world. Since the creation of the cosmos, God has reigned over it. Though I have had no religious belief, I feel that God is and see God's work now at this moment.

The incredible sight gives me a thrill of fear. I feel as if I have been swallowed up into the white mountains, although I stand firm.

TRANSLATED BY S. KURAMOCHI

5.

The Approach to Japanese Sanctuary

Yasuko Iwasaki

****

The churches I have visited in Europe have Gothic spires which soar up into the sky: St Stefan in Vienna, the Cathedral in Milan, the Matthias Church in Budapest and the St Vitus Cathedral in Prague.

The spires of Sagrada Familia in Barcelona, Spain, still seem to continue extending up into the sky, exactly as envisaged by the late Antonio Gaudi. Its eighteen big spires, I am told, will be completed in the twenty-first century.

We cannot talk about European culture and leave Christianity out of the equation because church plazas have played an important role in the culture. When I looked at those churches, which have no trees around them, I could not help but remind myself of the churches in Japan.

In contrast, the shrines and temples in Japan cannot be separated from the nature that is around them such as woods, approaches and gardens. The external appearance of our five-storied pagodas in their precincts is in harmony with nature rather than soaring into the sky. Even a small shrine in a village is generally found in a grove.

We find serenity and peace of mind when surrounded by trees. This condition naturally leads us to pray, sometimes to pray to Nature. At Hitaki Shrine in Kumano-Nachi, which I once visited, the object of worship is Nachi Waterfall itself.

On passing through the shrine archway, I heard the roaring sound of the waterfall and found the stone pavement in the grove wet with mist produced by the spray of the falls. As soon as I passed the approach in mist, I faced the waterfall. The water flowing through a primeval forest cascaded 133 metres down the precipice in a long straight line. Overwhelmed by a sense of the divine, I looked up at the falls. I felt an enormous sense of oneness with the ancient Japanese who revered the waterfall.

The Meiji Shrine in Tokyo although located in the midst of the busy city, is surrounded by the forest of Yoyogi. The annual open-air Noh play dedicated to the shrine on 10 October is an amazing spectacle – performed as it is in the solemn but inspiring environment provided by nature itself. On that night, the long gravel-paved approach is lined with bonfires up to the Noh stage in front of the auditorium. The dampish night air and the briskly burning fires never fail to thrill the audience with the charm generated by Noh's light and dark.

On the stage lit only by bonfires, the Noh performers with their characteristic masks and costumes are clearly seen against the dark. The sound of chantings, tabors, drums and wind instruments breaks the stillness of the night as if to let the gods hear it. I experience the intensest delight in walking along the approach to the shrine, enticed to go farther into the depths and going back, soaked in the resonance as well as the elegant simplicity of Noh.

I have visited the shrine every year, sometimes invited by my son, at other times accompanying my husband and friends. When I visit foreign churches, I am particularly conscious of their spires, and at a Japanese shrine its approach leads me to feel I am getting closer to the gods.

The main buildings of the Grand Shrine of Ise, for example, are rather small and quite simple with well-ground tree ornaments on the roof, but the long gravel-paved approach surrounded with ancient trees makes the visitors feel quite pious as they advance.

The following old Japanese short poem accurately expresses the feeling that the visitors to a shrine have in its surroundings:

I cannot help shedding tears
Of blessing and sanctity:
What makes me feel so
I cannot tell, though.

TRANSLATED BY N. KUMABE

6.

The Snow-woman I Met on a Bus

Yasuko Iwasaki

****

One day in October, a cold wave suddenly hit Japan after a spell of lingering summer heat in late September. The cold stayed on until November. Early in November it was as cold as in December.

The changes of the seasons constitute elements which are indispensable to Japanese culture, but the unexpected confusion of the climate has not given me time to feel sentimental; instead it is causing me to fret about missing autumn.

The other day, my husband made a proposal:

'What do you say to making a day-trip on a bus to see "autumn" with our own eyes?'

I responded positively.

Every year, we have enjoyed travelling either abroad or in Japan. But this year the repeated dislocation of my hip joint, a fracture in my right wrist and a subsequent fracture in my left wrist have forced me to give up the idea of travelling. I cannot even walk without a stick, but a day-trip on a bus would be possible, we thought.

Now let me tell you about our trip. We left Shinjuku at 8.00 a.m. on a long-distance touring coach in which passengers have the use of two seats. Our destination was Kusatsu Spa in Gunma Prefecture. I was curious to know what it was really like having often seen on television the scenery around Kusatsu where the town is full of the steam from the hot springs.

When the bus left the midtown area of Tokyo, we were given a steamed hand towel, a tea-can and some sandwiches. This light meal tasted good and pleased me a lot since I had been very busy before leaving and had eaten only yogurt and a banana for breakfast.

At the time of our departure soft beams of sunlight were breaking through thin clouds, but thick clouds gradually came to cover a leaden sky as our bus travelled north. Despite my hope of seeing the scenery in autumnal tints, I saw nothing but desolate wintry scenes. After a while powdery snow began to fall across the bus windows. I heard the passengers complain:

'Oh, look! It has begun to snow at last!'

Just then the bus guide, who did not look so young, said to us:

'Excuse me, everyone. You may call a woman who always brings the rainy weather a "rain-woman". To tell the truth, I am not a "rain-woman", but a "snow-woman".'

The timing of remark rather puzzled the passengers, who did not see what she meant. They were already expressing a sense of unease.

'Whenever I work on a bus,' the guide continued, 'it always snows. That is probably because I come from Aomori, a well-known land of snow. I am very sorry for you. Today's snow is entirely due to me, a "snow-woman".'

She bowed low politely. The atmosphere in the bus quickly softened. The feeling that the weather cannot be helped went throughout the bus. My husband, who is always blessed with fine weather, could do nothing about it on this trip. I found it rather strange that the guide's remarks and bow had led me to respond positively to the unseasonable snow. Was it her quick wit to call herself a snow-woman in order to assuage the passengers' feelings? It cannot have been written in the guide's reference manual. My husband, who heard me whisper my opinion, said:

'I presume it was her own personality that prompted her to say that.'

If so, it was very considerate of her to make such remarks. Then I remembered that, after it began to snow, she took out a big thermos bottle and poured hot green tea into paper cups, handing one to each passenger. That also showed her considerate nature, I believe.

At Kusatsu Spa we were shown into a Japanese-style hotel more than a hundred and twenty years old. Our lunch, served on big Japanese vermilion-coated trays, was ready in the hall. The old hotel must have survived so long because of its stout wooden framework, although it creaked when heavy people walked around.

The bus was scheduled to leave at three. In the meantime the tourists made themselves at home; some enjoyed taking a bath in the hot springs; others went for a walk. Across the road in front of the hotel was a hot fountainhead spewing out an enormous volume of steam. Taking care not to slip on the road, I walked to a 'hot spring field', which is a famous symbol of Kusatsu Spa. The hot water, never boiled artificially, really comes from a hot fountainhead. They gather flowers of sulphur in the field. I also wanted to see 'rubbing hot water', another symbol of Kusatsu, where a group of people in a line stir the water of the hot spring with a board in order to cool it. The show, however, was expected to be performed after three o'clock, so we had to give up the idea of watching it and started back on our return journey.

Our little trip to search for autumn was rather disappointing, but what satisfied me most was that I met the bus guide who called herself a 'snow-woman'. As we approached Tokyo, it stopped snowing completely and the gathering dusk had a rosy-pink tint.

TRANSLATED BY N. KUMABE

7.

I Want to Become the Wind

Akiko Ohno

****

What is your favourite poem? To this question, I would cite an anonymous poem entitled 'A Thousand Winds'. I first encountered this poem about five years ago, in a newspaper column where it was introduced as a poem to comfort those who have lost their loved ones. The poem, already well known in the West, was read at the funeral of a British soldier who died in an IRA terrorist attack and at the memorial service held at Ground Zero for the victims of the 9/11 terrorist attacks.

The last sentence of the column, 'We do not know where and when this poem was born, so it's like the wind' stuck in my mind.

I wanted to know more about the background of this poem and to read the original English version. My wish was fulfilled in the book *A Thousand Winds* by Man Arai, a successful composer and author of music and lyrics. At the same time as publishing this book, he composed the music for the Japanese translation of the poem, sang it himself and issued a CD.

I read aloud the poem 'A Thousand Winds', a poem of only twelve lines at the beginning of the book. The words used are simple and I did not need a dictionary to understand the poem. Let me quote the first two lines:

'Do not stand at my grave and weep;
I am not there, I do not sleep.'

The eight lines that follow describe how I am now living in nature as the wind and the light and the snow. In the morning, I become a little bird and at night I become a star and look over you. The poem ends with the following two lines:

'Do not stand at my grave and cry;
I am not there, I did not die.'

Man Arai says he read the original poem aloud a number of times before beginning to translate the poem. The poem looks easy to translate but, in fact, it is somewhat difficult to grasp the meaning, but when he realized that this poem expressed 'rebirth from death', he says that the Japanese words came out smoothly. It is unfortunate that the end rhyming in the original poem is lost in Japanese, but I suppose it cannot be helped when translating into a different language.

In the part of the book called 'photo poem', each phrase is shown with a scenic photo expressing the image of the phrase. A green field, the sky with a rainbow, gold-coloured fallen leaves and the forest glittering with silver frost – it is as if we can hear the whispering of the dead from each scene. I am here. So do not grieve.

If those who cannot recover from a deep sense of loss could believe that their loved ones who have passed away are living somewhere in a different form, how comforted they would be.

Man Arai speculates that the author of the poem may be a Native American woman who believes in animism. He says that the author's concept of life being eternal is close to animism, which believes in the existence of spirits in all phenomena and all things.

I was attracted by this poem because I felt it had something in common with green funerals that I have been interested in for some time. Green funerals are funerals in which the bodies of the dead are not buried in graves but are cremated into ashes and scattered on the sea or in the mountains or buried at the foot of a big tree. These green funerals take place quite often in the West, in accordance with the wishes of the deceased. Ever since the Ministry of Justice authorized them in 1991 on condition that they are carried out 'within reasonable bounds', applicants have been increasing in Japan too.

According to a survey conducted by one newspaper, about 40 per cent of the people questioned replied that they did not want their remains to be buried in a grave. Most of those people wanted their ashes to be scattered on the sea or in the mountains where they have fond memories.

'I have no grave. When someone remembers me, I am there.' I deeply empathized with these words of a woman in her thirties because from time to time, I also remember my parents and friends who have passed away, see them in my mind and talk with them.

I lost many of my acquaintances in the last two years. They were all people who were quite well and active until only a few months before. As I am in my mid-sixties, death could come to me any time.

If I die without making my wishes clear, a Buddhist funeral will be carried out and I will be buried in the grave of my husband's ancestors in his home town. As I am not religious, I do not need a funeral ceremony, a grave or a posthumous Buddhist name. I want my ashes to be returned to nature and only my family need attend.

As I wanted to know more about green funerals, I called the NPO, Free Funeral Promotion Society, and asked them to send me their booklet. This society, founded in 1991, now has approximately 12,000 members. More than 1,100 green funerals have already taken place at sea or in the mountains. The board members of the society consist of scholars, lawyers, journalists and other intellectuals. To become a member, you have to send in an application form and pay 3,000 yen as an annual fee.

An important part of the activities of this society is the concept of the 'regenerated forest', the name given to the forest created by the contribution of the members. When the ashes are returned to the forest, the family of the deceased pays the fee for the maintenance cost of the forest. This is an attempt both to prevent the dilapidation of the forest and the destruction of nature in urban areas due to the construction of cemeteries. However, strong opposition seems to exist among people living near the forests. Some may feel it eerie to have human ashes scattered near their homes. I suppose many people still believe that burying in graves is the only way to part with the dead although scattering the ashes of the dead over hill and dale was an age-old Japanese custom and it was only in the Edo area that the common folk started to use graves.

In this way, there are both pros and cons for green funerals but I think that my husband and our children will honour my last wishes even if they feel a little bewildered. If possible, I would like to return to the mountain or sea that I visited with my family and friends. But no, I will not insist too much on the location. If I can become the wind as the poem says, I can go anywhere in the world.

I got lost at a resort last summer while I was on a walk. As I plodded on in the drizzling rain, the wind rose a number of times and whirled through the Japanese larchwood forest, up into the sky.

Was someone's spirit in that wind? I would like to become the wind someday.

TRANSLATED BY H. MIYAZAKI AND Y. TAKAHASHI

8.

In the Sunshine

Midori Sekiguchi

****

Now we have the cool weather at long last. Day after day I managed to survive the terrible heat, which lasted even after the autumn season started. Since it was too hot for me, a healthy person, it must have been an unbearably hot and long summer for my mother-in-law, who suffered from chronic tuberculosis. She breathed her last in her flat, where she lived alone, on the first day of the equinoctial week as if she could bear the lingering heat no more.

One of the main reasons why the lingering summer heat was unbearable was not only that we were exhausted because of the continuous heat, but also that the sunshine began to slant. In midsummer the sun shone just above so that its rays did not penetrate into the inner part of our rooms, whereas with the start of August the lower sun began to shed its slanting rays into the innermost recesses of our rooms and made the air that much hotter.

I realized this was also the case with the mother-in-law's flat, when I stayed there to nurse her.

Nothing blocked the view from the flat on the 7th floor, for there was no tall building, only a large park on this side of the block of flats. From the window of her living room, I could see Mt Fuji in the distance to the south-west. In the afternoon the slanting western sunshine relentlessly penetrated deep into the room from the large and wide picture window. The lace curtains were not enough to block the rays. Thick curtains were needed. Fortunately, her bedroom faced the north-east and was thus not exposed to the direct sunshine, but every room was full of hot air and the air conditioning was essential night and day. She died on the afternoon of one such hot day.

The following day, burdened with a heavy heart, I saw a beautiful sight in the western sunshine.

Having decided to go home, I left my husband in the flat and I went to the car park. I sat at the driver's seat and looked up, when I saw some gold-coloured things floating over the flower bed. They were so visionary that they looked as if they were in a framed picture. It took me a few moments before I realized that they were a mass of yellow butterflies dancing in the sunshine. They flew up and down airily like a vision.

I thought my mother-in-law had come to say goodbye to me. Then I remembered that I had dreamed such a dream some time before.

As a child I saw a great number of butterflies dancing in the sunshine over a flower garden on a hill. I pursued them, pushing aside the tall grass, followed by a dog and a rabbit who were playing with me.

I woke up with a feeling of supreme bliss, and told the family about my dream.

'I am sure you were in heaven, my husband said in a joking way, but I was willing to believe him, because the dream had really reminded me of a heaven.

Golden butterflies dancing in the sunshine over the flower-bed had gone upwards, while I felt as relieved as I did when I woke up from the dream.

TRANSLATED BY S. KURAMOCHI

PART 2

NEW YEAR'S CARDS

9.

New Year's Cards

Ayako Akutsu

****

One day, I received a postcard from Yuko, a friend of mine since my junior high school days. It was about her decision not to send a New Year's card. She said: 'Now that I have finished the most important work in my life, I have begun to think that the time has come for me to choose a more relaxed way of life. Accordingly, starting from next year, I will not be sending you a New Year's card. I would like to ask you in advance to forgive me for my lack of courtesy. I now wish to enjoy my life by doing only what I want to do.'

My husband and I send about four hundred New Year's cards, addressed not only to friends and relatives but also to those people related to my husband's company. It is a terrible burden to write them at the end of the year, when we have so much shopping to do for New Year's Day as well as a major houseclean. It takes two to three days to write all the cards. I have often thought what a relief it would be if I could stop sending New Year's cards.

On New Year's Day our letter-box, like everybody else's, is filled with greeting cards. I am happy to receive them, although it is troublesome to send them. While reading them one by one, I have a lively conversation with family members about what has happened to the sender's life.

Most of the cards just offer formal greetings, it is true, but some people proudly inform us of happy events such as the birth of their grandchild. Others use them for commercial promotions. Most people perhaps want to stop sending them, but hesitate to do so, since they are afraid they might fail in their social obligations if they did so.

When there was a death in the family, a simple postcard would arrive to inform us that the sender was in mourning for the deceased and that a New Year's card would not be sent. Consequently, I was shocked when I received Yuko's postcard before New Year's Day. I wondered who had passed away.

Actually nobody had died in her family. When I phoned Yuko, however, she told me that there were two contrasting responses to her notice. Some people were critical of her imprudence in deciding to stop sending New Year cards while she was still in her seventies and in good health. Other people admired her for her unusual courage.

I told her that I would be behind her. As the days passed, however, I felt a sense of loneliness, thinking I would never hear from her again and I had lost a close friend. Yuko and I were bound together in recent years only through exchanging New Year cards once a year

It is true that a New Year's card is only meant for sending greetings, but for us elderly people it is the means of assuring ourselves that our friends are alive and well.

I remembered many things associated with Yuko. She had lost her father in the war and was brought up by her grandparents – her grandfather was a doctor. They were too busy with their work, so she was left alone. She had read almost all the works from the complete series of world literature. She invited us, her six closest friends, to her room in her Western-style house, and explained the story she had just finished with gestures and in an excited tone of voice.

When I heard her talk about *Jane Eyre*, *Wuthering Heights*, *Rebecca*, *Manon Lescaut*, in the cool air of the room, I felt as if the house itself were the stage for the story.

When I was a junior high school student, I was not mature enough to properly understand what a love story was. Yuko was precocious. She explained what kind of woman a 'mistress' was and so on.

In addition, we had great fun there. The maid served us tea. In those days, soon after the end of the war, we suffered from a lack of food and were always hungry. A hot cake with honey, a slice of bread with butter and jam were so delicious that I could not believe such food really existed in this world.

Then I had the impression that for a doctor everything was provided, and was filled with envy. I think the six of us went there, attracted by the tea. How relaxed the junior high school students were sixty years ago! We developed a close friendship.

She was the first amongst us to marry. She may have longed for an ordinary family life. She loved and took good care of her husband and children. Even when we were grown up, we visited her for advice as she still remained a 'leader'.

I have not seen Yuko for a while now, although we spent much time together in our younger days. New Year's cards had been the only means of communication with her. The last tie was broken with a snap.

TRANSLATED BY S. KURAMOCHI

10.

At the Beginning of a Year

Mayumi Tomiyama

****

Visiting a Shrine on New Year's Day

I make it a rule to pay a visit to the shinto shrine near my house on New Year's Day. I have sometimes visited famous shrines on that day, but, as I have visited my local shrine on every important occasion, such as the traditional Japanese celebration of a newborn baby and that of a child's third, fifth and seventh birthdays, it has become so familiar to me that I always go there on New Year's Day.

We Japanese usually have noodles for dinner on New Year's Eve, because noodles are thought to be the symbol of long life. At midnight all the temples ring their bells, bidding farewell to the old year. When we heard the sound of the temple bells after having noodles, my husband said, 'Let's go, shall we?'

We then got ready to go to the shrine. Of course, we put on warm clothes to protect ourselves against the chilly night air.

It is a twelve or thirteen minutes' walk to the shrine. While walking quietly in the shadows, I wondered how many people would be in the queue in front of the oratory this year. As it was midnight, the familiar road looked quite new to me. On my way some groups of two or three people joined us in heading for the same place. The shrine is located at a section of a residential district. Its fine oratory stands on a plot of ground surrounded by a stone wall. The ground occupies approximately 2,300 square metres.

As I approached the shrine, I found a queue of people ahead of me. I stood at the end of the queue. I anticipated that it would take thirty or forty minutes to get to the oratory.

After paying homage we were given sacred saké, which was served in a small paper cup. I felt the cold saké sinking into my body. I joined the people warming themselves around an open-air fire which was burning charms of the old year. The flames leapt high producing sparks and crackling sounds. I felt a glow inside and outside, and then made my way home, wishing that this might be a good year for me.

New Year's Gift

On the second day of the new year, I paid a visit, as is usual every year, to my husband's parents' home in Hachioji, about a hundred kilometres west of central Tokyo.

As our car began to cross the Tama River, which borders Tokyo, my husband cried out, 'Oh, look! Mt Fuji!'

The magnificent view was of the mountain gleaming white clearly visible against the blue sky. I too enjoyed the surprise of seeing it even though it was more than a hundred kilometres away. It is really worthy of being called 'the highest and greatest in Japan'. During the first three days of the new year, the Tokyo air is far clearer than during the rest of the year, which might be the reason why it is easier to see Mt Fuji. Anyway, it was a rare chance to enjoy its startlingly beautiful view. Though the view was sometimes interrupted by tall buildings, my eyes constantly followed the mountain. I never grew tired of it. As I watched it, I felt my mind purified by it.

Since the road was not busy, we reached our destination earlier than we had expected. Just as I was addressing my mother-in-law, the four members of my son's family arrived. Akiko, a fourth-year student at primary school, said happily that she had seen Mt Fuji on the way. My son confessed that he was so absorbed in the view of the mountain that he missed his turning. We kept our New Year compliments short and spent most of the time talking about Mt Fuji.

My eighty-seven-year-old mother-in-law looked very happy when she gave her New Year's gift to her grandchildren, thanking them for coming all the way. She said:

'You can see Mt Fuji very well today from the veranda. Go upstairs and enjoy the view.'

On hearing these words Akiko and Teru, both five years old, determined to be first in running up the stairs. Mt Fuji was a little dimmer than it had been early in the morning, but the two children were overjoyed at the view.

The children, who typically spend their everyday lives without appreciating the scenery around them, were very happy to be given the chance to enjoy the sight of Mt Fuji. It must be the best New Year's gift they have ever received.

The Seven Deities of Fortune

A number of districts in Japan have their own Seven Deities of Fortune enshrined in Shinto shrines and Buddhist temples, to which the Japanese pay homage at New Year. On the third day of the new year, my husband suddenly suggested that we visit the Seven Deities of Fortune in Nihon-bashi. It is a place in the centre of Tokyo, well-known as the starting point of Japan's oldest highway, and has always flourished with people coming from all the parts of the country. We started from Nihon-bashi with a map which showed the location of the Seven Deities. A large crowd of people were walking in the same direction, so we followed them.

The first spot we visited was Koami Shrine dedicated to Fuku-roku-ju, the god of wealth and longevity. On arriving there, we were guided by a man who was saying in a loud voice:

'Those who are just passing by, please go that way. Those who wish to pay homage to the god, please stand in a queue here. You will have to wait for twenty or thirty minutes.'

'Merely to pass by?' I looked carefully and noticed that most of the people were walking on along the pavement after stopping for a moment to bow to the shrine with their hands clasped.

I followed the queue. A lady who looked a little over seventy years old was just behind me. She spoke to me as if she knew what I was thinking.

'Paying homage to every shrine after waiting in the queue for a while needs time and physical strength. Some of them, I hear, get a stamp only at the last shrine, and convince themselves that they have completed the tour of visiting the Seven Deities. I myself actually visit all seven places, waiting in the queue for a while at each shrine or temple. I believe I can get divine grace only by doing so. So many men, so many minds, you know.'

Her words were quite persuasive. Some people consider this visiting tour as a good walking for exercise. I went round the seven shrines and temples together with that old lady.

The next place I visited was Cha-no-ki Shrine, which means a shrine of tea trees. It was named so because it was surrounded by the superb green of tea bushes. The shrine is dedicated to Hotei, the god with a potbelly. The god's statue holds a big cloth bag on his lap. He is said to save the poor, taking treasures out of his bag. I prayed that he would help lots of people.

After my visit to Cha-no-ki Shrine, I walked along the main street and found the magnificent building of Sui-ten-gu, a temple sacred to the guardian deity of mariners. I had paid a few visits to it before, because it is well known for being responsive to prayers for the blessing of children and a smooth delivery. Benzaiten, the deity of fortune, to whom the temple is dedicated, is the only goddess of the Seven Deities. I especially prayed for my daughter, who got married the year before last.

After paying homage to three other divinities of wealth, treasure and longevity, I came to the last spot, Sugi-no-mori Shrine, which means the shrine of a Japanese cedar. The shrine is dedicated to Ebisu, the Mercury of Japan. A monument for the lottery, which was very popular during the Edo Era, stands in its precincts. After saying my prayers at the oratory, I followed suit with the people who rubbed the smiling monument.

I felt relieved when I completed the tour. I looked at my watch and found I had spent nearly three hours going round. Some of the shrines and temples had a magnificent building like Sui-ten-gu; others were dwarfed by tall modern buildings which surrounded them; still others were tiny ones comprising a rented room in a private house. All of them seemed to be trying to survive the ravages of time. I imagined what the Seven Deities felt about them.

I learned later that Ebisu, the Mercury of Japan, is the only deity that was born in Japan. The others come from India or China and are enshrined in Japan. When the Japanese worship, they are not scrupulous about whether the object is a natural god, or Buddha, or Jesus Christ. This lack of scruples has brought good luck and happiness to us Japanese. This thought made me feel happy as I made my way home.

TRANSLATED BY N. KUMABE

11.

The Day before the Calendrical Beginning of Spring

Kiyoko Nakajima

****

'It's really a long time since the last time I took part in the bean-scattering ceremony celebrating the coming of spring,' said my father happily, as he took down a bag containing beans from the family Buddhist altar.

According to the old calendar, 4 February is the end of winter. On the previous night, the Japanese hold the bean-scattering ceremony, by which they drive away evil spirits and welcome gods of wealth. These days, few families do this, but many shrines and temples choose lucky-bean scatterers and hold the ceremony.

On that night this year, I was at my parents' home in Kyoto. As he cut open the bag containing the beans my father said:

'When we lived in Ohtsu, all of our family enjoyed the ceremony of bean-scattering; it was great fun. I would hurry home from my work to be in time for scattering the beans to drive away evil spirits. You children would scatter the beans shouting so loudly that the noise must have annoyed the entire neighbourhood.'

He seemed to be enjoying reminiscencing. Since my mother died in hospital three years ago, my father must have been very lonely as he enacted the ceremony for the coming of spring on his own. My father, very faithful by nature, continues to scatter beans by himself.

In the days when we lived in Ohtsu, a city to the east of Kyoto, my mother used to buy beans in a measure of one-*go*, which correst-ponds to 180.4 cubic centimetres. She put the beans into an earthen pan of unglazed pottery and gently seared them over the heat. Her three children – my brother, sister and I – watched the process patiently around a briquette brazier.

When the beans were about to crack open, my mother put a wooden lid on the pan and shook it. When they started making a loud cracking noise, she removed the pan from the brazier, took off the lid and put the half-burned beans into a small bowl. Then she offered the bowl to the family Buddhist altar. The aroma of the baked beans was so tempting that my brother and sister would try to eat them before the offering was made and would be scolded by her.

After dinner, all the family went round every doorway and scattered beans, shouting in chorus:

'In with fortune! Out with demons!'

Our old house in Ohtsu was located near Miidera, a very famous old temple. The nature of the locality is seen in the appearance of the houses there; ours was no exception. The corridor, called a 'passage garden', constituted a passageway from the entrance to the backyard, and we could walk there with our shoes on. In the middle of the pathway, there was an oven, a sink and a gas cooker in a row next to each other, which made up a kitchen. The washstand and the lavatory were located outside, right by the back door, so that we had to go there in the very cold air about the time of the bean-scattering ceremony. But since our dog was kept in the backyard too, the location was very convenient when we took it out for a walk.

This is what happened in that 'passage garden' on one evening of the bean-scattering ceremony. After all my family had gone to bed, I heard a rustling and crunching sound coming from the 'passage garden'. I opened the window quietly and shone a torch into the gloomy garden. I noticed two squatting objects. They were two rats, nibbling scattered beans in their paws. They were innocently eating the beans. I was suprised, but they looked so lovely that I kept watching them for a while without driving them away.

From the next year on, the scattered beans were cleared soon after the ceremony. As the years passed by, we scattered fewer beans inside the house but more outside. Anyway, our family, which consisted of six members including my grandmother, continued to perform the cheerful ceremony of bean-scattering.

My father had gone upstairs before I was aware of it; he opened the windows of the rooms and began to scatter beans, shouting:

'In with fortune! Out with demons!'

My ninety-two-year-old father, now living alone, was taking the trouble to protect his house. I said to myself:

'Father, I'll come to Kyoto again next year.'

I joined him in scattering beans, just as we had done in Ohtsu, I scattered more beans outside, and fewer inside the house. I shouted as loudly as my father:

'In with fortune! Out with demons!'

TRANSLATED BY N. KUMABE

12.

Dolls Displayed at the Girls' Festival

Akiko Iwashita

****

According to the old calendar, 4 February is the first day of spring. A cold, wintry wind may still sweep through and it may sometimes snow, but the rays of the sun surely get brighter. On a particularly fine day, I decided to display dolls in readiness for the Girls' Festival in March.

The set of dolls I brought out had been given by my father to my only daughter for her first Girls' Festival. The complete set should have seven altars, but it was too large for my house with only two rooms and a dining kitchen. My father, therefore, chose to buy only the dolls of an Imperial prince and princess, so that we might add our own purchases later. The set of dolls was 150 centimetres wide. We were so pleased with it that we would work hard to decorate it while my daughter was very young.

It has been an old Japanese custom that families with girls set up altars on 3 March, the Girls' Festival, and decorate them with dolls, miniature household items and peach blossoms. They usually have lozenge rice cakes and white saké made from saké and rice malt, and we all pray for our daughters' growth and happiness. I like this Japanese custom so much that I have displayed the dolls every year, praying that my daughter may be happy. Our set of dolls did not include those representing three maids of honour and five musicians, which a full-scale set should have included. I prepared, however, a sweet drink made from fermented rice instead of white saké, and uncaked sushi served in a bowl, and clam soup in another bowl – the menu which was sure to please little children. I would display the dolls in good spirits, hoping that some day they would be put on a full-scale seven altars display.

I have to be very careful in handling the dolls and over the years it has gradually become rather a nuisance. Sometimes March draws near before I am aware of it, and I display the dolls in a flurry. I take them out of the boxes where they have been shut up in the dark for a year, and expose them to the spring sunshine. When I have been late in displaying them, I leave the dolls on the altar, sometimes for as long as a month after the Festival, so as to make up for my idleness.

My daughter, who was a high school student at that time, said to me at work:

'You should take out the dolls early and put them away early. If you are late doing that, your girls will be late in getting married.'

'Dolls should be kept away from moisture, so I choose a fine day suitable for displaying them. I should like to keep them in a good condition until you grow up,' I explained.

'But you set them up them quite late and leave them on the altar. I'm sure I'll be late in getting married!'

Such things might be discussed at a private high school where my daughter went. Nobody was interested in such a thing at school in my high school days. That may be because my high school was co-educational. Possibly in those days, Japanese society was still badly off in the post-war rehabilitation period and we had no time to talk about dolls.

Over the generations we Japanese have used such expressions as 'to send out a daughter in marriage' or 'to dispose of a daughter'. As a play on words, taking dolls in and out for the Girls' Festival may have come to imply giving a daughter in marriage. Anyway, I couldn't find anything to say in reply to my daughter at that point.

My daughter is now in her late twenties, and still remains unmarried. Is my idleness the cause of her delayed marriage? So, from now on I will take out and put away the dolls early, hoping she will come across a good partner in the course of this year at the latest.

TRANSLATED BY N. KUMABE

13.

Seasonal Change of Clothing

Yoshiko Obata

****

The cherry blossom season is over. The leaves of the trees which began to sprout in early spring have turned deep green. On the morning of a holiday at the beginning of May, I opened a window and felt myself bathing in the warm rays of the sun. I then decided to arrange my seasonal change of clothing, since I would not need heavy coats and sweaters any longer.

First, I took the heavy coats out of the cupboard and after inspection put them in a corner of the room. I make it a rule to send to the laundry those coats which I wore during winter. Next, I opened a chest of drawers and took out the sweaters I had also used during winter. In one pile I put those which I would take to the laundry for dry-cleaning. In the other I put those which I would wash at home. Then I opened the sliding door of a wall cabinet. In the boxes arranged in the lower partition were the summer clothes which I had put there at the time of seasonal change of clothing last autumn. When I took off the lids and put them on the floor, I found that the side of my mobile phone was flashing. I had not noticed that there was a message. I checked the phone and discovered that the message was from my elder sister in Kyoto. It said:

'I have been arranging my seasonal change of clothing since yesterday. I am sick and tired of doing it. Buying new clothes, of course, needs money, but now disposing of old ones also costs some. I've made up my mind never to buy another dress.'

Reading my sister's e-mail, I could imagine her sighing in a sea of clothing just as I was doing then.

My sister and I have been fond of dressing smartly since our childhood. Before we got married, we would go shopping not only in

Kyoto but further afield in Osaka and Kobe. After our marriages, our situations became quite different from each other. I have devoted myself to domestic chores, only sometimes working part-time. My sister has continued working at an office five days a week. She has often complained that as a commuter she constantly had to be dressed up and could not possibly go through even one winter wearing the same overcoat. Naturally she has also had the additional costs of spending money on her dresses.

Some years ago when she came to have time to herself, freed from looking after her children, she said to me:

'I went shopping on my own and bought this.'

In those days I spent most of my time doing chores at home. Except when I went out occasionally for my part-time job, I usually stayed at home. The opportunities for me to get dressed up were when I went shopping for food and when I attended a PTA meeting at my children's school. You might think that my principle of buying a dress only when I was entirely satisfied with it was a bit of a luxury. Recently, I stopped working part-time and started a new life as a regular worker. Since then I have been faced with a variety of situations requiring my presence when I have had to take care to choose a dress suitable for the occasion. This necessarily led to increasing the number of my dresses. Surrounded with piles of clothing, I sent an e-mail to my sister:

'You had better throw away the clothes you haven't worn for five years. However highly you may regard them, they are a miser's gold buried in the ground. Changes of fashion take place so quickly it makes five-year-old clothing out of date. It may be nothing but rubbish.'

Putting my mobile on the floor, I continued arranging my seasonal change of clothing. The T-shirts I took out from a chest have not been worn for three years. I remembered I had bought them at a supermarket bargain sale at the end of the season when my daughters were primary school pupils. Should I throw them away, or . . .? My attachment to them prevented me from making up my mind to throw them away. I didn't wear them last year, it is true, but I might put them on this year. Finally, I decided to keep them and put them into the chest. Next, I took out my sports wear. The colour was a little washed-out, but I might wear it at home. I thought I had another one quite like that, but I looked for it in vain.

I got so tired of my work that I decided to have a break and telephoned my mother:

'This kind of work is really tiring. We know we should throw away many of the clothes, but . . .' said my mother, who always does the same thing as I do. The following is what she went on to tell me.

When my father was dead, my mother disposed of many of his clothes, but she still retains some for the sake of his memory. She also takes good care of a particular kimono which she had been given by my grandmother. Once a year she has to dry it in the shade lest it should be worn out. This time of the year when we have a refreshing breeze is the best time to dry a silk kimono in the shade where it does not get direct sunshine. If she neglects the work, the result is that the graceful silk kimono is damaged by mould or vermin. Worms seem to know what tastes good to them. It takes a few days to finish the work of arranging the seasonal change of clothing. In the end my mother said with a sigh:

'I know the clothing that I have at home is enough for my use. Still, I feel like getting some new things to wear occasionally. We are destined to seek luxury, aren't we?'

Three women – my mother, sister and I – are sighing while they are engaged in arranging the seasonal change of clothing. We do this job four times a year at every turn of the season. I sometimes wish I could live in a land like Hawaii, where you do not have to be bothered with seasonal changes of clothing. But it would be boring never to enjoy the change of the seasons. That is what I am thinking about.

TRANSLATED BY N. KUMABE

14.

Kimono – from Mother to Daughter –

Kazuko F. Fujino

****

On a fine day towards the end of May, I open the chest of drawers every year to replace winter kimonos with those for summer. It is now the time of the clothes change for the summer season.

I check those lined kimonos I wore more than a few times in winter and take them to the kimono shop to get the neck-bands, sleeve-bands and the bottom of kimonos cleaned.

I prepare unlined kimonos to wear in June, silk gauze and gossamer for July and August. I wonder, how many times I will be able to wear them in the hottest season, but I place them on top of the kimonos in the drawers, to make the silk gauze and gossamer easier to take out, as my mother used to do every year.

When I got married, my parents ordered all the necessary kinds of kimonos required for different occasions. They included *hohmongi* used for visiting or party-going, *edozuma* which married women wear at the wedding breakfast of relatives, and *mofuku*, a black kimono with family emblems used for mourning. There were also other kimonos for daily use, for summer and winter.

At that time, my mother hand-made a quantity of undergarments with bleached cotton cloth. 'Nowadays young people don't wear kimonos so often; these may be enough to see you through your life,' she said.

She put aside the kimonos I had worn before my marriage and kept them with her, saying, 'They are too colourful and bright. I will alter them for you after dyeing them in better colours.' But she must have had too many memories of my young days to change those kimonos. She took them out from the chest and gazed at them by herself again and again; she did not take them to a dye house.

My parents were not so rich as to order new kimonos easily for my mother. When my father forced my mother to go and buy her kimono, she would change her mind while selecting one for herself; she usually found one for me and ordered it. 'Look. How beautiful! It will be just right for Kazuko.' My mother came home happily with a box of cakes and undershirts for my brothers, while my father appeared not to be in full agreement. My mother must have had many wishes for me as her only daughter; she could not easily forget her dream.

When I gave birth to my first daughter, Mari, my mother said, 'Mari will soon grow up and be able to wear those kimonos,' pointing to those kimonos of mine she had been keeping with her. She looked forward to her granddaughter wearing them, even though it would be many years later.

After a while, complying with my husband's advice, I again started learning the tea ceremony. I went to tea gatherings, wearing kimono. I needed kimonos which I didn't have to worry about spotting with tea during training. I asked my mother to send my kimonos she had kept so that they could be altered. They were red or pink, already nearly twenty years old then.

Twenty more years have elapsed since then. I'm still wearing those red or pink kimonos. Probably I will go on wearing them all my life.

Since my childhood, perhaps according to my mother's preference, I was dressed in a fine kimono on New Year's Day. I was puffed with prickly heat powder after my shower and was made to put on *yukata* in summer evenings. She used to say: 'You are my only daughter.' I would have preferred to wear short pants and run round with my elder brothers.

I didn't forget the day when I had my *furisode* made. When it arrived, my mother took off her apron and called me joyfully. 'Come here and have a look!' She opened a large flat envelope and removed the thin wrapping paper. It was my *furisode*. Mother unfolded it carefully and put it over my shoulders.

It had a pair of long hanging sleeves from the shoulders almost reaching the floor. The cloth was white satin filled with woven-in chrysanthemum patterns. It had traditional multi-coloured wave patterns on the lower part. They were embroidered with gold, silver and many other coloured threads. It was really beautiful. My mother said. 'After all, my choice was best, wasn't it?' She looked satisfied. I wore it for the last time at my own wedding breakfast.

Furisode is the formal dress for unmarried women. To be precise, one's own wedding breakfast is the last opportunity to wear *furisode*. When my first daughter grew up, I had my *furisode* altered to fit her. She wore it when attending the wedding breakfasts of her friends.

It is a big event for parents to order *furisode* for their daughters. It is very expensive. Recently, many young people have decided to wear a rented *furisode* for particular occasions but they do not know how to wear it and have to go to a dresser. Fortunately, I can put on kimono by myself, because I saw my mother wear kimonos by herself in daily life. My daughters have learnt to wear kimonos by themselves by watching me wear them.

My mother died at the age of seventy-three. Many of her kimonos were left behind still with basting thread. It was only after my marriage, that my mother began to order her own kimonos. My father sent all of them to me. I would remodel them for my size and wear them myself, ensuring they would be suitable for my age.

Kimonos are handed down over generations, carrying with them the memories of the preceding owners.

TRANSLATED BY THE AUTHOR

15.

A Good-luck Charm

Hiroko Yamada

****

I generally stop at a shrine or temple when I come across one while travelling or going for a walk. Those places usually have a stall, where good-luck charms in colourful packaging meet my eye. Charms never fail to remind me of an episode I had while my son was a senior high school student.

His high school always held a parent-teacher meeting in their classroom twice a year. At one particular meeting I reached the school a little too early before the meeting started. One mother saw the name-tag I was wearing, identified me and spoke to me:

'I am a mother of a friend of your son's. I know your son is quite religious. I feel there is something rather strange about that.'

Her remarks were so unexpected that for a moment I was dumbfounded. I asked her:

'What makes you think so, may I ask?'

'My son tells me that your son always carries a lot of good-luck charms with him in his bag,' she replied.

'Dear me! I had no idea.'

'Didn't you know that? The fact is that my son has changed a lot since he made friends with yours,' she continued. 'Recently, my son paid a visit to a shrine or a temple and got a charm there. Since then he has made it a rule to go to school with the charm in his bag. He has become much gentler in his nature than he used to be. What makes me especially happy is that his results have improved at school.'

Soon afterwards we seated ourselves and the meeting started. Most of the time was spent on the teacher's report about school events.

A few days later, I ventured to ask my son, who was in a good mood because it was a holiday:

'Do you always carry charms with you in your bag?'

'Oh, how did you know that? Did you look in my bag?'

'Your friend's mother told me about it at the parent-teacher meeting a few days ago.'

'Now you know! How embarrassing is that!'

My son was shocked to discover that a high school student should reveal his friend's private secret to his own mother.

'When did you begin carrying charms with you in your school bag?'

'When I was a junior high school student.'

'Why did you start doing that?'

'Partly because I wanted to pray to the Divinity or the Buddha for help, but the real reason is that my grandparents often gave me a number of good-luck charms. I was so moved by their kindness that I started carrying the charms with me.'

My parents would be very glad to hear that. Next time I saw them, I would tell them about it. My son went on:

'The problem is that I now have a huge number of charms. I decided to limit the number I carry to two or three; but it takes so much time to choose them. The result is, I carry more than twenty with me, and my friend found out.'

After that, we never referred to charms again. After finishing high school, my son went on to a university. Now he is a businessman and has two children.

Only recently my son talked about charms. Smiling, he said:

'I know my parents present charms to my wife and children just as my grandparents did to me. Is this a family custom?'

Certainly, I gave his family a charm for a smooth delivery, seven centimetres by three centimetres long, made of a beautiful textile, and another for good scholastic achievements, and still another for good health.

My husband and I are in our sixties, and so share the same feeling that my parents had at that age. I feel that packed in a charm are not only traditional Japanese prayers to the Divinity or the Buddha but also a loving parental consideration for their successors.

TRANSLATED BY N. KUMABE

16.

A Year Like Any Other

Sachiko Mibu

****

For nearly twenty years, we have had a family get-together on New Year's Day in order to have dinner at the same Chinese restaurant in the same hotel. This included our family of four, my sister's family, also of four, and, until three years ago, my late mother-in-law. This particular restaurant offers an all-you-can-eat style menu as a New Year's Day special, where, for a fixed price, the guests can order any number of dishes of their choice.

When the children were young, they would try to order familiar dishes that we always had at home, and my sister and I would try to change their minds saying, 'You should choose something more expensive today. What about lobster?' And our husbands would protest saying, 'Oh, let the kids have what they want.' After making our choices in this way, the children would each tell us their resolutions for the year to come amid cheers and questions from the others, a little embarrassed by the attention they were getting. This has gone on year after year.

Some years my sister's family was abroad and was not there, or we were on a trip ourselves on New Year's Day. But this get-together must have become imprinted in the children's minds as an institution because even when they were going through a rebellious stage as teenagers and didn't want to go out with their parents, or when they had been drinking with their friends through the night on New Year's Eve, they all turned up for this New Year's dinner.

For me the dinner had become an annual event that I took for granted, something I enjoyed without giving it any particular thought. My mother-in-law, however, had always looked forward to this annual dinner with special relish perhaps because she dined alone most of the time. The New Year after her death, I realized for the first time that this event, which I had taken for granted, was not going to go on for ever.

In Japan, a family does not usually celebrate the New Year following the death of a family member, but on that New Year's Day we got together as usual and had dinner at the same Chinese restaurant. A person who should have been there was missing; nevertheless, conversation was as animated as usual and everyone ate as usual with great gusto. I wondered whether this was how life goes on.

This year, our son who had married the year before brought his wife and their baby, and our five-month-old grandson became the centre of attention. My niece, who is working in the US, joined us with her fiancé. They were getting married in Japan in the spring, and everyone made suggestions on where they should go for their honeymoon. Enjoying this lively scene on New Year's Day, I was suddenly seized with the fear that it was not going to continue forever, and the fear remained in the corner of my heart. My mother-in-law is no longer here today, and someday . . .

In the last few years, many of my friends and acquaintances of my age have died or have become seriously ill. Perhaps this is to be expected when you are in your mid-fifties. A friend's husband who was full of life the day before is now lying in a coma after a cerebral hemorrhage. Another friend who had just begun to enjoy taking trips with his wife fell ill and died. Yet another is now fighting an illness and suffering from the side-effects of her treatment.

I often become obsessed by the feeling that it must be my or my husband's turn next. Illness creeps on you unawares and attacks you out of the blue. It seems to me like a nightmarish game of dodge-ball, in which you don't know where the ball is coming from. It would be impossible for a person with poor reflexes like myself to dodge the ball. This thought makes me cringe with fear.

Maybe because of this thought, I could not fully enjoy the peaceful New Year's dinner, and I felt all the more strongly that this was something I did not want to lose.

Why do the Japanese make so much fuss over New Year? This is something that has intrigued me since childhood. In the stories about

Japan in the past, we read that even very poor families used to get new underwear and prepare a sumptuous meal on New Year's Day.

From writing our New Year's cards, preparing various New Year's dishes and rice cake soup to at least showing the semblance of a general house-cleaning and stocking up on some food – since getting married, New Year had become, in fact, the busiest season of the year for me and I couldn't wait for this period to be over.

But this year was different. I felt so happy that we were able to welcome the New Year safely. I now understood the special meaning of New Year's Day and why the Japanese people have handed down this feeling of celebration from generation to generation.

May this year pass safely, without any untoward happenings. May it be a year like any other.

Feeling a little tipsy from the Chinese rice wine and looking around at the family members who were sharing this meal, I made this wish from the bottom of my heart.

TRANSLATED BY H. MIYAZAKI AND Y. TAKAHASHI

17.

The Day of Farewell

Asako Ono

****

It was the morning of a warm Sunday, 22 February 2004. I wanted to get up late as I usually do on Sundays, but my dog's bark asking for breakfast forced me out of bed.

'Today, I have to take out the stored dolls for the Girls' Festival in March,' I said to my dog which was hungrily eating its food. I vaguely thought I would invite my parents and my husband to our Doll's Festival the following week.

Three days before the day, I had telephoned my mother. She sounded in low spirits. She had visited her sister in hospital. While she was taking care of the patient, she was told upsetting things by her sister's eldest son to the effect that she was intruding in other people's affairs. That came as a great shock to her. She complained that she had been unwell since then. She said in a fit of anger that I did not have to visit my sick aunt. I attributed it to my mother's parental affection, but then I remembered the case with my grandparents and another relative. When they were dying, my mother advised me not to visit them, which caused me not to attend their deathbed and made me feel sad. That memory led me to say:

'The decision to visit my aunt is for me to make. She is much advanced in years now. If she dies before I see her alive, I'll blame you for depriving me of the opportunity to see her.'

My words added to my mother's depression.

On the day before, I was going to see my mother and apologize for saying too much, but the sudden decision to dine out with my family prevented me from visiting her. So on that Sunday I thought I should go and see her to talk about the Doll's Festival.

The telephone rang. When I answered it, I heard my father's voice. He never calls me unless he has some important matter concerning my mother. I felt an inauspicious resentment.

'Mother's awful. I've just called for an ambulance. She said she felt sick, and fell down after vomiting.'

'Is she conscious?'

'No.'

'Oh, my God!' I felt a cold sweat coming from my hand as I held the receiver.

I woke my husband and daughter. I knew I had to rush to the hospital although I had no idea where it was. Further information would reach me as I drove north on Loop 7. My daughter, a junior high school student, was in our car within five minutes; it usually takes her half an hour to get ready to go out. My husband had already started the engine. I pushed my dog into the car and then got in myself; I didn't have any make-up on either. The dog was barking uneasily, perhaps conscious that something quite unexpected had happened.

My mobile phone soon rang. I learned that my mother had been taken to a hospital in Nakano.

'Grandma is all right, isn't she?' my daughter repeated, but I couldn't give her an answer. Since my mother was far from being robust, even slight symptoms of her poor health caused anxiety to the people around her. I was always a victim of that anxiety. As her only daughter, I had begun to feel uneasy about losing her even when I was a little child. I also felt I must be prepared for it. When I heard my father's call, I knew instinctively that I must really be prepared for the worst. My husband drove faster.

The doctor diagnosed my mother's condition as acute myocardial infaction. She had died almost instantly, although the ambulance men's life-saving action brought my mother back to life for a while. I was shown to her sickroom. She was laid in her everyday wear, and had her face covered with a white cloth. My daughter burst into tears.

Taking away the cloth, I saw her closed eyes, and then what she had said three days before over the telephone came back to me.

Wasn't she urging me to come and see her at once? I was so sorry to have misread the situation and become irritated with her. I should have gone to see her even late at night instead of dining out with my family the day before. The result was that I put myself in the dreadful situation of not attending my dear mother on her deathbed.

I recalled a similar scene in a drama I had seen. Everything must be a nightmare, I said to myself. In a dream I was still in bed, feeling comfortable in the warm air of the morning, and expecting to be roused by my dog's barking. Tears overflowed on my lashes.

I can't recollect what happened afterwards. I dimly remember that the doctor explained that an autopsy would be required because of her sudden death. I have completely forgotten how and by what route I returned to my parents' home in Koenji. I may have had some *onigiri* someone bought at a convenience store. I may have arranged the necessary arrangements for the funeral with an undertaker.

I notified all the relatives and every person I could think of that my mother had passed away, using her address book and the New Year cards she had received. I chose a picture of my late mother from her album to be used at the funeral. I felt some strange force driving me on to take such actions.

I followed my father to pay a visit to our family temple in Suginami. We were gently welcomed by the chief priest and his wife. We asked him to give my mother her posthumous Buddhist name.

'She is seventy-nine years old? I am afraid she is too young to pass away. I hear she is interested in quite a number of things,' said the priest to comfort us. The fact is that for over twenty years my mother had been developing her talent as an artist doing Japanese paintings. My father told us that she had been awarded a number of Tokyo Governor's prizes and newspaper publishing companies' prizes.

My mother's posthumous Buddhist name was Shomyoin-Kashitsu-Koei-Daishi, which signifies that she continued to draw pictures for a long while.

It was completely dark by the time the police handed over my mother's corpse and laid it in a room in the temple. On my way home I stopped at the approach to the temple to admire the peach trees in full bloom. They looked proud in the light of the outdoor lamps. The sweet smell of daphnes was floating in the air there.

Why were the flowers blooming so beautifully even though they had no one to draw them? I really missed my mother, who had always been with me in my daily life. She passed away in a hurry without hearing a word of apology from me.

The reality which I did not wish to recognize penetrated relentlessly into the core of my mind. For the first time in my life I saw my father shedding tears. And the coming spring would be the first one when the Girls' Festival would arrive and I would not be displaying any dolls.

TRANSLATED BY N. KUMABE

PART 3

PLEASE ANSWER IN JAPANESE

18.

The Living God

Atsuko Shimakawa

****

This is the sixtieth year since the end of the Second World War. Our country has transformed itself as if by magic its following miserable defeat in the war. Now it has been regenerated into such an economically rich, democratic and peace-loving country that we could never have dreamed of six decades ago.

What follows is the story of an unforgettable event which took place some years after the end of the war and the image of a scene I observed then is vividly etched in my memory.

When I was five years old and the Pacific War was yet to break out, I was separated from my parents and sisters living in Tokyo and moved to the countryside in Ehime-ken, Shikoku Province. During the war I was brought up by my grandparents.

The war ended when I was in the fifth year of primary school. On New Year's Day of the following year the Showa Emperor publicly declared that he was a human being and renounced his divinity.

When I was at the junior high school, I heard that the Emperor, whose presence had never been revealed except as a portrait photo, was travelling throughout the country in order to meet and talk with the people personally.

One day, I heard that he was coming to our province. The fact was that the Imperial train was just passing through the railway station near our hamlet, without stopping. On that day the school was to be closed. Our classroom teacher said to us: 'You can go to welcome him, if you wish, but each well-wisher is expected to be courteous and good-mannered.' Most of us hesitated to go, perhaps because our teacher's words made us nervous; but I, a curious girl, was willing to have a look at him.

It was my grandfather that was most excited at the news. He said, 'What a gracious thing! I will go to the station and worship him', and began to do something or other to prepare for the occasion. To him the Emperor still remained a living god. In fact, every morning he turned his face in the direction of the Imperial Palace, clapped his hands and bowed deeply.

First, he obtained some new straw and carefully made a straw mat. He had his hair cut at the barber's. On the previous day he told his wife to prepare the only formal wear he had, a *montsuki-haori*, or a Japanese half-coat bearing the family crest, and a *hakama*, or a Japanese man's skirt, *tabi*, or Japanese socks, and *geta*, or sandals made from the wood of an empress tree, and to arrange the complete outfit in order by item in the alcove.

On that day, he got up early and heated the bath. When my grandmother and I got up, he had already taken his bath. I was told to take a bath to clean myself, since I was to accompany him.

None in the neighbourhood went but my grandfather and I. We were dressed in formal wear, holding a rolled new straw mat. As far as I remember, the train was to pass at about ten o'clock in the morning, but we arrived at Nyuugawa Station on the Yosan Railway two hours before.

My grandfather chose a piece of ground near the railway as a place of worship. He was afraid we would be disrespectful to the Emperor if we knelt on the platform, because there we would be almost level with the royal seat. The lower we knelt, the better it would be.

We unrolled the new straw mat which we had brought with great care. We took off our wooden sandals and knelt side by side on it. We waited patiently for the moment to arrive.

Suddenly, the people around us stopped chattering. The Imperial train was coming through, slowing its speed. All the people bowed. The train passed.

I bowed, but I cast an upward glance at the Emperor. I clearly saw him. He was waving his white-gloved hand. When he was just in front of me, my heart beat quicker; I didn't know why. I was suddenly filled with a feeling of awe from head to foot, realizing he was such a great man and, as had been believed, to be a god. My grandfather bowed so deeply that his forehead almost touched the mat. He never lifted his face until the train was gone.

On the way back he remained silent perhaps because he was tired.

'Our teacher tells us that the Emperor is not a god any more,' I said.

'He is absolutely wrong. His Majesty the Emperor is a living god,' he replied in an accusing and affirmative tone.

In those days people were unsophisticated and conservative in that rural district, which was blessed with a mild climate. The villagers respected the schoolteachers and just believed what they said, but for once my grandfather flatly rejected what our teacher had said. I was at a loss for words to answer him back. I kept silent and sympathized with him.

Since his childhood my grandfather had been brought up in a society where the Emperor was worshipped as a god. He could not easily accept that the Emperor was just a human being and that the idea of his divinity was not true, despite the fact that this country was defeated in the war. I said to myself, 'I myself feel uneasy somehow, unable to adapt myself to the rapidly changing ways of thinking and living, although the pre-war thoughts are not so well fixed in my mind. I had better let him think as he pleases.'

'You are tired, aren't you, Grandpa?'

'I'm all right, dear. I got up a bit too early this morning, though.'

He was the gentle grandfather once again.

Ten years after that, in 1957, he died at the age of eighty.

TRANSLATED BY S. KURAMOCHI

19.

Hiroshima

Katsuko Oka

****

8.15 on the morning of 6 August 1945. That is the moment when an atomic bomb was dropped on Hiroshima. I was thirteen years old.

At the time, I was in the schoolyard in the city of Kure, about twenty kilometres from Hiroshima. Suddenly, I felt a blast of hot air on my right cheek and imagined myself gently floating. A boom immediately followed. Then I saw the 'mushroom-shaped cloud' from a nuclear blast. A clear light-pink cloud, as if mixed with whipped cream, swelled up into the sky. It gradually disappeared, its colour changing from pink into sepia and then into dark brown. Of course I had no idea then that it was caused by the atomic bomb dropped on Hiroshima.

At that time my uncle and aunt were medical practitioners at a hospital a hundred metres from the epicentre. A number of patients were already there that day, waiting for their turn to be examined.

It was not until the evening that we learned what had happened in Hiroshima. As the hours passed, thousands of the injured escaped to Kure, our city. They told us that the bomb was of an entirely indescribable nature.

'Are our uncle and aunt safe?' I asked.

'They haven't let us know anything about their situation. Which means they are safe,' said my mother explicitly, although she looked a little anxious.

Two days passed, but we had no communication with them. On the morning of the third day my mother determined to visit them, taking lunch, some water and a parasol with her. The following is what she told us later.

It usually took an hour to go from Kure to Hiroshima by train, but the bombing had caused all the train services to stop. Instead, she got a lift from a passing lorry driver who took her to Hiroshima. The Hiroshima tram network extended throughout the city with the tram terminus located at the railway station. Far more of the city was destroyed than my mother had anticipated. The trams had completely stopped, of course, but in front of the railway station were a considerable number of people who had managed to get there in order to enquire after their relatives' safety.

My mother had to walk to our uncle's, following the tram track. It was the only landmark left for her, because all the buildings were entirely destroyed and she had no way of knowing which direction it was.

Seven rivers flow through Hiroshima, so it is called the 'city of rivers'. As my mother walked along the tram track and crossed a river, she found the damage to the city was worse. Several reinforced concrete buildings were all that were left; they were severely damaged and just empty shells.

Ai-oi-bashi, a bridge close to the epicentre, was a beautiful bridge famous for its unusual 'T' shape. Its parapets had all fallen off, and a soldier on horseback lay dead at its middle. My mother flinched at the sight of a charred woman whose feet still retained the trace of her white socks, and urged herself to walk on for a further five minutes from the bridge to our uncle's hospital. That short distance was covered with piles of debris and she had no idea where the road was.

She managed to reach the hospital only to find it deserted and desolate. She saw about thirty dead bodies at the entrance. She wondered if one of them was our uncle. The sun was exceedingly hot and she felt very thirsty. She could do nothing. Her parasol was the only thing that protected her. The heat was stifling and all that she heard was the noise of the wind. She sat down on a hot stone in front of the building, wanting so much to see someone alive.

It was noon. She kept waiting in the hope that someone would come.

'Kiyoko-san! Aren't you Kiyoko-san?' She heard someone calling her by name.

It was an old man, one of her relatives, who had come from a faraway village, accompanied by a few people. He had a shovel in his hand and said:

'I came here yesterday, too, but could not find any clue as to their existence. Today I've got these people to help me to go further inside what was left of the building. Let's go together.'

My mother, however, shook her head and said:

'I'll wait here.'

She could not help shrinking back. After a while she saw the old man beckon to her from the inner part of the ruin, saying:

'Come here! I've found them! Take care to step only on the foundation stones, or you'll get burnt.'

Our uncle's hospital was an ultra-modern building in those days, but there was no trace of its original form. She had to pass by the dead bodies lying there which seemed to be those of the patients. She went further inside with utmost care.

There on the ground she found our uncle and aunt. The couple lay face to face with the distance of a table between them, which made you suppose they were having breakfast at the time of the bomb blast. All that remained of their bodies was the skull, the thick shoulder bone and the jaws. Beside them were plates with a striped pattern of dark brown and white, which they always used.

'Their skeleton tells us who they are,' said the old man.

'Certainly,' my mother nodded.

She did not remember how she got home, she told us later. It is generally thought that the American plane attacked Hiroshima because the Japanese military headquarters were there. We could not help thinking that the two hundred thousand citizens of Hiroshima would not have been victims if the war had ended nine days earlier.

The only thing that consoles us is that my uncle and aunt would not have suffered an agonizing death because they were very near the epicentre and were killed almost instantly. Also the couple departed this life together by themselves at 8.15 on that day. Had they begun treating their patients, they would not have been easily recognized in the midst of so many victims.

TRANSLATED BY N. KUMABE

20.

'I Want a Japanese Bell'

Miki Hamane

****

When I was working as a Spanish interpreter, I happened to make the acquaintance of Maria, a woman who was working at the Embassy of Ecuador. She loved Japan and Japanese things. She learned how to do the tea ceremony, how to arrange flowers and how to make pottery. Above all, she had an interest in Buddhist temples, and whenever she was free; she took her camera and happily visited temples in the Tokyo area.

Unexpectedly, she was ordered to go home because of a personnel reshuffle and had to leave this country after only a year's stay. In the remaining days she wanted to fulfil various wishes. She climbed Mt Fuji and bathed at a hot spring. I accompanied her on both trips, adjusting my schedule to her busy one.

Three days before her departure, when I thought she was very busy, she called me and asked me to help her buy a souvenir which so far she had not been able to find. She wanted to obtain it by whatever means, but she did not know where to get it. In Hiroo, a central district in Tokyo and a high-class residential area with foreign embassies, where she lived, she seemed unable to find it.

She said, 'I want a Japanese bell.' I immediately thought of a wind-bell, a bell which hang at the edge of the eaves and tinkled in the wind refreshingly. It would be a good present from Japan.

'No, not that kind of bell. I want a little bell which sits on a small cushion on the altar of the temple.'

Oh, my! I thought, she means a rin gong on the Buddhist altar.

'I have never heard such a beautiful bell sound.'

Listening to her with my ear to the receiver, I was taken by a strange feeling. I knew that a rin gong rang with a rich tone, as she suggested, with its high-pitched clear sound and lingering reverberation, but to describe the sound as beautiful was beyond my imagination.

A rin gong is one of Buddhist articles used in funeral ceremonies and other Buddhist services. Usually priests strike it when they chant a sutra to mark a pause. Therefore, to us Japanese that sound is associated with death and reminds us of sad and painful memories. Or it is nothing but an unpleasant metallic sound because we were forced to sit in a correct manner and listen to it in our childhood.

While I was absorbed in such thoughts, Maria said to me urgingly, 'Could you tell me as soon as possible where to buy it?'

'All right. I will find out.'

Without thinking much about the task ahead I said I would, but I had no idea where the Buddhist articles were sold. I managed to find a friend who knew where the shop was. I asked her to accompany us to it the next day.

She took us to the busy traditional shopping arcade. Both sides of the straight street were crowded with so many different kinds of shops selling goods to meet all aspects of our daily lives. We found a particularly impressive shop with a glazed façade. There was a wide space inside the shop. On three sides different kinds of Buddhist articles, such as household altars of different designs, incense burners, candlesticks, vases and so on were displayed. We found rin gongs in a glass case. There were many sizes – between a whiskey glass and a salad bowl – and materially different ones, for example, gold or silver. She asked for six of the same size – as large as half an orange, which was the normal size.

All of them tinkled refreshingly and reverberated around the shop.

'What beautiful sounds! I'll take them all.'

'Are you sure, Madam? All of them? Thank you very much indeed. One moment please. I'll wrap them up.'

The grey-haired elderly shop owner answered with a winning smile and took a grey-coloured paper from the cash register stand.

Slightly discontented, Maria said: 'Haven't you got a bright colour? I prefer a red colour.'

'You know, we sell Buddhist items in this shop. We don't have bright-coloured wrapping papers. But just a moment, please.'

He rushed to the Japanese confectionary shop next door, and brought back pink papers patterned with cherry blossoms.

Wrapping them carefully one by one, the owner asked Maria why she wanted as many as six.

She answered that she would put one by her bedside to soothe her into sleep. She would put another in the hall to cleanse visitors, and she would give the rest to her close friends as a souvenir.

'Is that so?'

That was all the owner said. He was at a loss for words. I was also at a loss. I was dumbfounded by her quaint plan. I suspected she had no idea on which occasions those bells were used in this country.

Maria was not the first foreigner that puzzled me in that way. I had often been struck with admiration, although mixed with embarrassment, at many other foreigners who had such an unusual idea that we Japanese would never think of. For example, some of them would often use kimono as a bed cover and *obi* (or belt for kimono) as a table runner. Others used lacquered chopsticks as a hair accessory.

It was the first time, however, that Buddhist articles such as a rin gong would be used for other purposes, but I thought there could be many ways of using such an article. It would be all right if it was carefully and wisely used, although not for the original purpose. Used in a unique way it would please people of different countries and races.

TRANSLATED BY S. KURAMOCHI

21.

Please Answer in Japanese

Akiko Ohno

****

'Why do Japanese people answer in English when I talk in Japanese?' I read this question in a reader's column of a newspaper. It was posed by a British person who had been living in Tokyo for a long time.

I have lived both in Europe and the US myself, and encountered various experiences regarding language. So I understand both the feelings of the writer and the feelings of those Japanese who reply in English in spite of themselves.

The simplest reason is probably because the Japanese person wants to speak English with someone from overseas.

An American friend of mine told me that when she was enjoying a quiet, solitary trip around Kyoto and Nara, she was constantly assailed by junior and senior high school students wanting to talk to her in English. She found it quite annoying. I am sure they only wanted to try out the English they had learned at school to see if they could really communicate. Even grown-ups going to English conversation schools or following English language courses on TV may not be able to resist trying out their English if they happen to come across visitors from overseas.

Another most likely reason is that Japanese people have a perceived notion that it is impossible for foreigners to speak Japanese well.

Japanese is a complicated language. It has three types of script, the Chinese characters and the two syllabic scripts, hiragana and katakana. The written language and the spoken language are very different, and so are polite language and regular language. Even the Japanese find it difficult to use honorifics properly. So the Japanese can't help thinking, 'If it's difficult for us, what must it be like for foreigners?'

Japanese is also a language with many special features. In his book *The Japanese Language*, the linguist Haruhiko Kindaichi clearly explains the characteristics of Japanese in comparison with other languages. For example, no one asks a Japanese person, 'What language do you usually speak?' Wherever you travel in Japan, you need not worry whether Japanese is spoken in the region or not. This sounds obvious but it isn't. Belgium has two official languages and Switzerland has three official languages, and in both countries, different languages are spoken in different parts of the country. Apparently, a country like Japan where only one language is spoken throughout the land is quite rare in the world. Another characteristic of Japanese is that we are able to communicate in Japanese throughout Japan but nowhere else.

Because of these characteristics, the notion of Japanese as a language of the Japanese people and a language of the country Japan is firmly embedded in our minds. So when a Japanese person cannot speak Japanese or when a foreigner can speak and write Japanese well, we can't seem to accept it right away.

I was once speaking in English with a friend from Hawaii, an American of Japanese descent, and encountered cold stares on trains and in restaurants. People seemed to want to say, 'If you're Japanese, why don't you speak in Japanese?' But though this friend looks Japanese, she can speak hardly any Japanese.

On the other hand, when Hideo Levy, an American novelist and scholar of Japanese literature, came to Japan for literary research in the late 1960s, people told him that it was impossible for a non-Japanese to become a creative writer in Japanese. But later on, he was awarded the Noma Literary Prize for New Writers for a novel he wrote in Japanese.

The Japanese are not unique in this. The Dutch are also convinced that foreigners cannot speak their language. When I was living in the Netherlands for three years, I studied the Dutch language and tried to use it in town, but I always got replies in English. I knew my Dutch was poor but I used to wonder why they didn't at least acknowledge my effort and reply in Dutch. Because of that, my Dutch did not improve at all.

I used to think that as Japanese is a minor language, we have to learn English to join the international community. As Japan has become an economic power, however, the number of people learning Japanese in the world has continued to increase, with about 2.4 million people now studying Japanese. Whether Japanese is complicated and special or not, people are finding that it is a language worth learning. Let us get away from the preconceived notion that it is impossible for foreigners to speak Japanese.

Still, we can't expect to communicate in Japanese everywhere in the world. If we are going to live in a country for a certain period of time and work there, it is only a matter of courtesy for us to learn the language of the country.

In the world of sport, Japanese baseball players have begun to succeed in Major League Baseball, and football players have also started playing in the European club teams. But when they are interviewed by the local media, they are, for the most part, accompanied by an interpreter. I always feel that they would be able to communicate much better with their team mates and supporters if they could speak the language of the country.

To the people from overseas living in Japan, I would like to say: 'If you are going to live in Japan, do learn Japanese.' But it is impossible to expect tourists and those on short business trips to speak Japanese. So to be able to communicate with these people, I want as many Japanese people as possible to learn to communicate in English, which is now the acknowledged international language.

Since reading the reader's column, my rule of thumb in communicating with people from overseas is this: try to reply in Japanese if spoken to in Japanese, and in English if spoken to in English.

TRANSLATED BY H. MIYAZAKI AND Y. TAKAHASHI

22.

What is Taught in Japanese Language Lessons

Yuriko Yoshihara

****

I have been teaching Japanese at a private girls' high school for nearly twenty years. This experience has convinced me that the Japanese language syllabus not only aims at teaching the Japanese language but also plays an important part in developing 'a Japanese mind'.

I lived in Beirut, Lebanon, as a primary school pupil, and studied in the English class. The other students were from the US and more than ten other countries. Most of the textbooks were American; those for 'Reading', 'Writing' and 'Poetry by Wordsworth' were thick and splendid in appearance. Most of the time was spent in English lessons. At the age of ten, I felt attached to Shakespeare by reading his masterpieces and by reciting his poems. But we were not taught about the minds of the characters in his plays, which, I presume, was due to the fact that English was not the mother tongue of most of the students; we were taught to grasp the meaning of the words and the outline of the story. The questions in the textbooks were not about the minds of the characters. Even primary school students were expected to understand the masterpieces through the complete acquisition of the faculty of speech.

In Japan, on the other hand, literary works are studied in depth. When we deal with those works, we take great interest in trying to understand the minds of the heroes and heroines'. The textbooks never fail to include questions about the characters' minds. The teachers are expected to encourage the students to share their opinions. Of course, the study of a particular novel may produce conflicting opinions and we may not reach a definite conclusion. The teaching of the Japanese language in Japan, I feel sure, aims at letting the students share the minds of the characters in literary works.

Twenty years ago, the students had little difficulty with comprehension, but those in the present class cannot read and understand deep psychological analysis. One reason may be that the social trend towards the nuclear family where parents are too busy at work to teach them how to give due consideration to others. Another reason may be their growing accustomed to the exaggerated world of animated cartoons.

I remember a class in junior high school in which I introduced a certain novel as a text. The story is set in an ordinary Japanese home of forty years ago. The hero is a fifteen-year-old boy, whose home is actually a simple family store dealing in dry provisions. During the rainy season all his family become quite nervous, because the dry provisions sold at the store can be quickly infected with vermin or go mouldy. In such conditions, his mother says unpleasant things to his father who loafs on the job and gets into an argument. The boy, trying to avoid getting involved, earnestly lends a hand with the housework and tries to think of something to say which will please his father. His grandmother also helps to lightern the atmosphere by cracking jokes. The tense atmosphere in the house is gradually relieved by their efforts, and the family sit at table for dinner in the usual peaceful way they do every day. The boy feels a weight has been lifted from him. The story is very common and can happen in any home in Japan. Since ancient times the Japanese have set a high value on a capacity always to be concerned about those around them. We, the middle-aged, have naturally acquired such a sense, which the children of the present age find difficult to understand. This may be because children are left alone at home while both parents are out working to earn a living. Many years ago, children used to behave themselves to please their parents, but these days the situation is reversed. Parents spoil their children by attaching the greatest importance to sending their children to excellent schools. This reality has increased the number of students who find it difficult to relate to other human beings.

The following is what I experienced when I taught *Botchan*, a novel by the famous Japanese novelist Natsume Soseki, who was born in 1867. It is a very interesting novel that Soseki wrote while he was young.

In his childhood, the hero is naughty and unyielding, and often annoys his family. When his friend asks him if he can jump from the top floor, he does so and is then unable to stand up. When his father makes fun of him for what he did, he says nonchalantly that he will jump properly next time. The humour in the story, however, is not understood by today's students.

My former students would read the story and laugh at the humour, but the students these days do not see what is so funny. The Japanese are losing the spirit of *Rakugo*, a traditional Japanese art of the comic story. They are generally thought to be very serious, but during the Edo Period they really had a good sense of humour. They had a sense of being warm-hearted and never intentionally causing hurt to others. Then I introduce other literary works and give further examples of good Japanese traditions. In that way, the students come to understand what I mean and I feel relieved at their reaction.

This year, I taught the senior high school students *The Tale of Genji*, the masterpiece of Japanese classics. It is a thousand-year-old long novel – the oldest in the world. The story of Hikari-no-Kimi, or the Prince of Light, a brilliant young noble, and the young beautiful ladies of gentle birth around him, fascinate today's readers. I believe its length, depth and multiformity is unparalleled in the world. Its close description of various types of the feminine mind shows the writer's surprising powers for detailed observation. When we read it aloud, we feel its beauty, loveliness and sadness penetrate our minds. And this deep emotion makes up the very essence of the Japanese aesthetic sense, which is too difficult for students to understand at first. As they continue to read the classics, however, they become aware of the charm and meditate on the happiness derived from sharing the tradition of the classics.

I know a lot of people are of the opinion that more time in the Japanese classroom should be spent promoting discussion and writing essays that would be useful in the context of everyday life. But I should like to bring up students who are able to share the same feelings and points of view articulated in the past as well as the present.

TRANSLATED BY N. KUMABE

23.

Should Convenience be Taken for Granted?

Keiko Bando

****

On returning from work and checking the letter box, I found an 'unable-to-deliver' notice from the Post Office. I called them up at once and was told that they would redeliver the package right away. It was already six-thirty in the evening and they were going to deliver my post tonight. How the Post Office has changed! I was astonished. This must indeed be the effects of privatization. Ten or more years ago, I remember we had to go to the head Post Office of the area ourselves to retrieve any packages that could not be delivered in our absence. As I found this a nuisance, I remember asking people not to use the postal package service when they send me things.

I also remembered a talk given by the founder of a private parcel delivery service about ten years ago. On receiving a phone call from a client, this delivery service picked up and delivered parcels within a day of the call being made. The man repeated many times: 'Our company has been successful because the services offered by the Post Office, a governmental body, are extremely poor.' The Post Office thus criticized then was now offering the same services as the parcel delivery service.

A little after eight o'clock that same evening, an elderly delivery man came to deliver our parcel, a trip he had made exclusively for us. At the sight of this conscientious-looking man, a thought flashed through my mind. Hasn't the improvement in the services of the Post Office caused him to miss dinner with his family?

Japanese companies have developed and prospered by fulfilling the self-centred needs and desires of their clients. Convenience stores are open twenty-four hours a day and many supermarkets are now open for business even on New Year's Day. Some banks and even municipal departments offer services well past seven o'clock in the evening. Everything is decidedly more convenient and comfortable.

But . . .

But this has meant a heavier workload and more irregular hours for the workers. At times like these, when employees are wary of corporate downsizing, no one complains about long working hours. At the same time, the needs and desires of the users and consumers are boundless. In no time at all, convenience becomes a 'necessity'. I wonder if the little bit of convenience people are getting actually ends up taking away time and happiness from other people.

The package that was redelivered was a study kit for our son, who is still in primary school. I knew that my consideration for the postal worker is not going to have any effect on how things are, but all the same I regretted my decision. I wished I had waited until the following day to have the parcel redelivered.

TRANSLATED BY H. MIYAZAKI AND Y. TAKAHASHI

24.

Nuclear Power Plant in Earthquake Country

Toshio Iwaki

****

The earthquake in Niigata that occurred on 16 July 2007, which was named the '2007 Chuetsu Offshore Earthquake', caused great damage to people's lives and property. If you look back, over the past twenty years we have had twenty examples of big earthquakes that caused great devastation inside Japan. The damage (50,000 people dead and injured, 250,000 wrecked houses) of the earthquake in January 1995, known as the 'Great Hanshin Earthquake', sounded a warning which told us just how frightening it is when an earthquake happens directly above its epicentre in a big city. Among these natural disasters, the one I am particularly interested in caused damage to the Kashiwazaki nuclear power plant during the Niigata earthquake of 2007. The reason for this is that I used to be involved in the safety of a nuclear power plant, working as a design engineer for the nuclear reactor and responsible for the safety of the power plant.

Although I have never been in charge of any Kashiwazaki power plant work or earthquake-proof designing by myself, through the process of filling in the application form for safety inspection, I have had some experience with these kinds of technical situations. This is why I think that the safest buildings in Japan today are nuclear power plants.

Most places in Japan, whether on land or sea, are near active seismic centres. Also, the record shows that we have had more than 130 earthquakes which have caused great damage in the past 100 years. This is why we have been careful to avoid active faults, which is where an earthquake originates, when we select a site for a power plant. Next, the foundation of the reactor is built by digging into the bedrock below the ground and using reinforced concrete. With earthquake-proof construction designed to meet the most stringent safety standards as our top priority, we keep planning and analysing the architecture and the machinery. Moreover, we ensure our calculations are correct by mock-up-testing using large machines that simulate earthquakes. However, the earthquake in Kashiwazaki of 6.8 magnitude emerged from a fault which we hadn't noticed when we chose the site for the nuclear power plant compound. It was, in fact, a bigger quake than the limit approved by the safety inspectors for earthquake-proof construction.

Nevertheless, at the Kashiwazaki plant, all seven nuclear reactors were successfully shut down. Also, the radioactive leakage was negligible directly after the earthquake and there was almost no negative impact on the environment outside the plant. There are three rules a specialist must follow in an emergency: 'To stop the nuclear reactor', 'To cool off the reactor', and 'To trap the radioactive waste', and all were successfully handled at that time. In reality, the damage to human life happened not in the nuclear plant but outside where fires started in the built-up areas.

Even so, this earthquake created a painful problem for people who were involved in nuclear power plants.

As regards nuclear administration, there is certainly a question of how to make use of this experience to improve the earthquake-proof, safety inspection of the nuclear power plant guidelines. Last year, in September, new inspection guidelines for earthquake-proof construction were put in place. When assessing faults, the old guidelines said that we had to reconstruct an image of how the fault appeared 5,000 to 10,000 years ago. In the new guidelines, however, we are supposed to go back 120–130,000 years. The reaction to an earthquake taking place directly above the epicentre has also changed. Under the old guidelines, it states: 'Hypocentre magnitude 6.5'. In the new guidelines it states: 'Hypocentre magnitude 6.5–7.2'. The power companies have to reinforce and remodel the plants that are below the standards according to the changed guidelines, but it is problematic because the guidelines that are essential are constantly changing.

Now I will tell you my personal story. The house I am living in today is thirty years old and made of wood. Several years ago, I went through the earthquake-proof inspection according to the government recommendation, but the result was slightly below the recommendations. So I did some reinforcement work and passed the standard. Soon after this the standard changed again and in March of last year I was told for the second time that the house was below earthquake standards and had not passed. According to the research of earthquake physics since the late-twentieth century, more and more earthquakes are happening around the world. Even in Japan, we have at least one big earthquake a year. However, I don't feel like remodelling my home at the age of seventy-seven. I believe that when an earthquake comes, whatever will happen will happen. I made up my mind to accept my fate.

In Japan, there is a traditional way of ranking scary things: 'Earthquake, thunderbolt, fire, *oyaji* (old man)'. Now that the feudal system has gone, the word *oyaji* no longer appears on the list. Even for the earthquake, which is supposed to be greatly feared, we think: 'Whatever will happen will happen.' In a natural disaster, we help each other and there are many people who recover from it. Such national characteristics have a tendency to have negative impact as far as our social development is concerned, but this is probably wisdom that we learnt from our natural environment.

I hope the day will come when we can share our knowledge with the world. Now that we have developed a nuclear power plant that can survive a big earthquake, we can surely disseminate the knowledge to other countries. By using the experience of the Niigata earthquake, I hope that we can help the world.

TRANSLATED BY P. HALTMAN

25.

Watch Your Step

Kaori Yamamoto

****

A richly-toned gong of the Buddhist temple made me open my eyes slightly. I saw the fresh foliage of a maple tree through a wide-open window. The morning sunshine, which had been barely visible minutes before, now had the vividness of early summer. A small grey frog I had found before I started my Zen meditation was still sitting under the tree. With its eyes half open and not moving at all, it seemed to be imitating me. The first stick of incense had burnt, which showed half an hour of meditation had passed.

Six or seven years ago my son, Akira who was then a student of a Buddhist high school, leaned against a chair after dinner and began to talk.

'Our director told us at the morning meeting what each of us owes entirely to our parents. Those parents were brought up with good care by our four grandparents. And those grandparents were brought up by our eight great grandparents. When you trace your lineage back in this way, you will find you are connected with all the people in the world.'

I watched Akira's face without saying a word. In those days Akira was absorbed with practising football as a member of his club. At the school festival he strummed his guitar as part of a rock band, shaking his head on the stage in the gym. How often I tried to inspire him, referring to the fable 'The Ant and the Grasshopper'. His talk about the morning meeting seemed to sparkle like a diamond. About that time I started to become interested in religious faith, although I had never thought of it except at marriages and funerals.

I chanced upon the Kei Temple while I was out for a walk one day in March.

The temple was so completely surrounded by a bamboo thicket that I could not see it properly from the road. It stands almost hidden in a plot of ground occupying about eighty thousand square yards. The Buddhist priest who guided me was kind enough to show me every tea-ceremony house dotted around the grounds. Those houses were not equipped with electricity, so the interiors were pitch-black unless the dormer windows were opened. At the end, the priest took me to the hall for Zen meditation, which stood deep in the recesses of the grounds. His small eyes were gentle behind black-rimmed spectacles.

'About thirty people, including a few women of course, take part in the early Sunday morning meeting for Zen meditation. They clean the hall after meditation, and can get home before nine o'clock, so that it minimizes disruption with their schedules on Sundays.'

The priest fully understood that I might be anxious about participating in the activity. Religious meditation has been one of the most important training courses for Buddhism since it was introduced from China eight hundred years ago. I knew it opened the door only for the male society, especially for male priests. Would I be allowed to take part in it? The sign on a little board located at the entrance of the hall read: 'Watch Your Step'.

I asked the priest the meaning of the words and was told that we should pursue our own minds and never ask others to give us spiritual awakening.

The dusk of early spring had already fallen when I left the temple. I expressed my thanks to the priest, but I hurried home in the dusk, thinking that I was about to start something very serious.

While I remembered those things in meditation, the first stick of incense burned out, and all the participants stood up at the sound of the gong. We walked around clockwise on the large floor of the hall covered with *tatami* mats. We moved quietly with both of our hands laid one upon the other on our breasts. We walked about ten minutes to let the blood circulate through our stiffened bodies.

Another rich tone of the temple gong was the sign to light the second stick of incense. We stopped walking, sat down cross-legged on our flat Japanese cushions, and started meditation again. This second round of meditation is the last course, during which the priest goes around with a flat fifty-centimetre-long stick in his hand. When he finds that someone has fallen asleep or is moving, he warns them by slapping them on the shoulders. Once I was slapped because I moved up and down a little while breathing deeply. He must have made an allowance in slapping a female participant. His slap made a loud sound, but I did not feel much pain.

Whether you feel the thirty minutes' meditation is long or short depends upon the degree of the depth of meditation. When your mind keeps perfect composure free from idle thoughts, you may be in a state where thinking is completely suspended. Then you are in a world of nothing, without any time or consciousness.

You feel extremely pleasant. Right at that moment, the richly-toned gong brings you back to the real world.

One night, a party for enjoying the full moon was held at the meditation hall, and all the participants were served simple cakes and green tea. The leaves of the maple trees, lit up by the lamps in the garden, were tinted red and looked very pleasing in the dark.

A senior male participant who sat beside me had been engaged in the practice of meditation for twenty years. Patting his knees, he grumbled in a low voice:

'Meditation is very hard for me in winter. As I continue sitting, I do not feel the cold any longer. My toes become entirely numbed.' I was so amazed that I cried out, 'You are bare-foot even in winter!' I learned that I need more training in Zen meditation.

TRANSLATED BY P. HALTMAN

PART 4

CALL ME MUMMY

26.

My Days with Our Autistic Son

Hitomi Ishiwatari

****

Call Me Mummy

I always wonder where to start when talking about our son.

Although I was already at a late child-bearing age according to old standards and had my share of maternity problems, our son born at 3780 grams was a picture of health. He breast-fed well, ate his baby food well, walked at ten months and it looked as though he was growing into an active, robust boy.

Once outside, our boy would go all over the place not allowing his mother to hold his hand. He never gave a glance to the children his own age in the sand box but took off his shoes and got covered with sand from head to toe. He would enter and exit the lift in the apartment and ride up and down in it without tiring of it. He was absorbed by television or the video at home. He was able to operate the remote control with amazing ease. He came running when I called out 'Snacks!' but never even looked back when I just called out his name.

Although we were bothered about his late speech, we were first-time parents who were somewhat optimistic while being at the beck and call of our son all day long.

So, I became pregnant with my second baby without any second thoughts. I went to stay at my parents' home in Yokohama for the birth in order to be under their care. It was during these three months that my mother and sister had doubts about the way our son was developing. My mother raised four children and my sister was right in the middle of raising her three children. These two experienced women spotted the truth about our son with so much more insight and accuracy compared to myself who was at my wit's end raising my first child.

'He is too different. You had better take him to a specialist.'

I returned to my home in Shizuoka and had our son examined by a paediatrician.

A tall, male doctor talks to me peering intensely with intimidating eyes behind a pair of spectacles. 'I think it is a mild case of autism. Although he is not typical in that he shows expression and mimics words and actions, one characteristic of autism is imbalance in various aspects of of his development. In your child's case, he has sufficient development in terms of motor ability but he is slow in his emotional ability relating to other human beings.'

So, it was autism, after all. Strangely, I felt better.

'Right now, he needs plenty of positive stimulation. He should play with his mother a lot,' the doctor said and for the first time his eyes were laughing. They were the kind eyes of a paediatrician.

'Fund a Widdle Foe . . .', 'Found a Little Fall', lyrics to a well known song.

Our two-year-old son was singing while tapping the rhythm on an open book with a fan. He had been fascinated by a five-minute song programme on TV called 'Everybody's Song' from a while back. The lyrics are shown at the bottom of the screen. He put the back of his hand to the screen, holding his pointing finger horizontally and traced the words. He seemed to learn words that way with his eyes and his ears. It dawned on me to buy him a text for the programme with the words and the music. His eyes shone. He started to sit before the TV set with an open text when the programme started and I had noticed that he was already in position with his fan in one hand.

He fanned me away at any slight attempt on my part to sing along with him as though telling me to go away. The singing lessons were self-teaching sessions with the TV set with no space for a parent to squeeze into. The fan which was tapped all day was soon worn out with the bony framework showing. The only task of the parent was to exchange it for a new one.

The television set, which sends out one-way information, was his only friend; it can be handled with ease by our son who prefers not to mingle with other people. The only words on his lips were words learnt from TV: Panasonic, NTT, Honda, etc. When he met his new-born sister, the words which came to him were 'A new product!' even if it happened to be a coincidence.

Our son continued to mutter advertising phrases as if to extend an invisible barrier surrounding him. He started to read the alphabet and the kanji. More than anything, wasn't he going to call us 'Mummy' and 'Daddy' just once? His mother's small wish seemed to grow as she looked at the back of the tiny figure facing the television set.

In the spring when our son turned three, our family moved to Tokyo and we visited School M which is an institution exclusively for autistic children.

'We will observe the condition of your child and give him suitable individual instruction. Let us find him a place where he can feel safe and we will take our time in guiding him so that he will gradually begin to listen to the teacher's words. We won't force anything on him. If he cannot be separated from his mother, his mother is welcome to come into the room with him.'

I was immediately relieved by the interview with the director of the institution who had a round face and gave the impression of being a kind lady, and I thought I could commit the care of our child to her.

The playroom I entered with our son had a trampoline, a slide, many toys, picture books. Arranged on the wall were hiragana and alphabet charts as well as handwritten pictures of an H logo for Honda and a Mitsubishi logo, etc., which were sure to make him happy.

There were five other boys of our son's age playing with women teachers one-on-one. Nobody minded my presence with my toddler daughter. They quietly continued jumping on the trampoline and turning over the pages of their picture books. The children were like magnets repulsing each other. They kept to themselves without any mingling as though to avoid even the touch of another body. It was a strange and lonely scene.

It was not only instruction for the children but also studying for the parents. My moment for relief was brief thinking we were OK once we got here. Meetings with the teachers were held a few times a month and each time I was taught what autism was about. Autism is an innate disability of the brain still being unravelled. It is a communicating disability apart from intellectual ability . . .

Does that mean he will never get well? Why our child? Is there a reason for it? I seemed to be drawn into the darkness without answers.

However, one day, the director gave us the following talk:

'It is said that autistic children are born at a rate of one in a thousand births. It is only because you are working so hard raising these children now that the rest of the nine hundred and ninety-nine mothers are enjoying normal child-raising. In other words, you are raising the autistic children as representatives of a thousand people.'

Inspiring thoughts came to me after listening to the talk.

We were chosen by God.

Our son's name 'Moto' is written as 'a desired person' in kanji. Our child we named so came to our house at God's wish. He was a gift from God! God chose us thinking these parents can do it, they can raise him. Being able to think this way, I became light hearted as though the bottom of my heavy heart was scooped up with a jerk by the two hands of God. Just with that bit of realization and pride, I was able to save myself.

That's right. I had no time for despair. Our child who could not even communicate well with his own mother was forced to live an anxious life all alone. How could I find a way of communicating my feelings to him if not through understanding the real feelings of a boy who shut himself up in his own world and seemed to act just as he pleased? His mother had a lot to learn. The important thing was not the problem of language but the communication.

Despite all of this, I still wanted him to call me 'Mummy' some day. I did not want to give up.

The day arrived suddenly when he was almost four years old. When my husband and I just kept on sitting at the table after dinner, our son came to us. He gave me a straight stare with wide open eyes and said, 'Mummy'. Well, he seemed to be making a formal confirmation in a rigid tone rather than calling me. Next, he stared at my husband's face and said, 'Daddy'.

'We seem to have our parenthood acknowledged at last.'

We looked at each other and laughed. As I was laughing, tears ran down my face. On seeing that, our son asked bewilderingly, 'Water . . .?'

'These are tears. Mummy is crying.'

Then, what did he do but fetch a piece of tissue paper and wipe off my tears, just as his mother had done for him.

As he was doing so he said, 'Come on! Come on! Try your best!'

I could not help but hug our son saying, 'You're right. We should try our best, Moto,' At which he quickly escaped from my arms as though he was being tickled and went back to play.

Millennium Birthday

It looked as though a shining gold tangerine was lazily floating on a sea of clouds. Sunrise! The date was 29 September 2000. The day we were starting at an altitude of ten thousand metres was Moto's fourteenth birthday.

Ten years had passed since Moto had attended School M, exclusively for autistic children. Moto had a little brother as well and there were three children in the family.

Although for the six years of elementary school, Moto was able to go to a normal class in the local school supported by the warm understanding of the local people, he went onto a special class after graduation. He had developed intellectually in his own way but there were problems with development in his social abilities, as was expected.

An incident occurred when Moto and I participated in the first class reunion three months after graduating from his elementary school.

'Do you think Moto's dream will come true?'

His former classroom teacher's words took me back.

Moto had written in his graduation writings that, 'My dream is to go and see the Sydney Olympics.'

At the climax of the Olympic Games on 28 September, Moto and I boarded the night-flight to Sydney, leaving behind my husband and two children. For Moto, travelling overseas was a first, of course, but this was his first aeroplane ride as well.

Take off! He was stuck to the window gazing at the night view below with everything becoming smaller and smaller so that it ended up looking like a map. Even after the flight reached cruising speed, the plane rattled and rocked when it went through turbulence. Every time that happened, Moto would look around with panic.

After a while, the first in-flight meal was served. Moto must have been hungry but for some reason he was not interested in it. He was wearing a drawn expression.

'Are you sick anywhere?'

'Umm, here,' he placed a hand on his forehead.

Having his first flying experience, either from becoming too nervous or maybe due to the change in atmospheric pressure, Moto seemed to be suffering from travel sickness which was not normal for him. After returning his meal, I covered him with a blanket. To my relief, he was soon asleep as usual.

While I was unable to sleep well because of being so squeezed up, I noticed the outside of the window had started to shine orange.

'Look! Sunrise!'

I called out to Moto who had woken up.

'............'

Remaining silent, Moto turned his gaze to outside the window. If it were our second son, he would have been very chirpy saying something like, 'Fab!' Moto did not possess words to tell us what was inside his heart. By thinking of how our second son would respond, I was coming face-to-face with this child's handicap again.

The air sickness turned out to be nothing serious and Moto ate up all his food after a good sleep and regained his usual spirits.

On landing at the airport we became acquainted with two girls on the same tour. We decided to take lunch in the hotel's restaurant with them. Delicious-looking shrimps and raw oysters for which Sydney is famous were laid out. Eat as much as you want for just 2000 yen, only half of what you would pay in Tokyo! We immediately made a toast with Australian wine celebrating Moto's birthday.

On noticing that, the waiter brought us a birthday cake with two candles on it! On the white plate were the words 'Happy Birthday' written in chocolate . . . I had never dreamed that Moto would be able to blow out his birthday candles so far away in Sydney! However, it was only me who got excited and Moto blew out the candles with an unaffected air and silently kept on digging into the Sydney buffet.

The Olympic Games Attending Tour was supposed to have got us seats for the track and field events, the soccer finals and the closing ceremony at the main stadium. Although it was a group tour, getting to the stadium was down to us to organize using the municipal train.

That night, we watched the track and fields events. Moto was unusually quiet beside me while I was getting all excited seeing Marion Jones right before my eyes.

After the games ended, we joined the queue of still exhilarated people heading for the station. Many attendants who we learned were volunteers were supervising the queue.

'I have a stomach-ache.'

Moto suddenly said and hunched over in the middle of the queue. Had he eaten too much lunch? Was it food poisoning from the shrimps?

I explained our situation to a nearby attendant and inquired about a taxi stand.

'It's sure to be quicker on the train,' he answered.

Another attendant soon brought us a wheelchair. He intended to put our son in it, wheel him to the train platform by the lift and then get him priority to board the train.

'I'm so sorry this has happened, but actually although our son has a mental handicap, I brought him from Japan because he had said he wanted to see the Olympic Games!'

The man who caught me sighing despite myself while waiting for the train said:

'Don't worry. We will all help you.'

Wherever he goes, our son would be helped and protected by everybody. The thought warmed my heart.

Moto's dream had come true thanks to so many people. They were the teacher who rooted for his dream, our family who sent the two of us off and the people we met in Sydney . . . It was the best birthday present ever.

Luckily, his stomach-ache had gone away by the time we reached the hotel. He must have been tired. Moto was fast asleep within fifteen seconds.

I took out a can of beer from the fridge and pulled opened the tab.

Outside the window, the neon lights of Darling Harbour spread like a sleepless castle. There were shadows of cars and a flow of people even after midnight.

'We really came, didn't we . . .'

Muttering out loud with my face on the window pane, tears welled up.

It had been a long, long day.

Our autistic son is growing up by accumulating experiences of days like these. The emotional thrill is everlasting because of the very fact that he is autistic and this is the source of my energy for life.

TRANSLATED BY ATSUKO BABA

27.

A Charm in the Morning

Fumi Ishii

****

A young mother in the class wrote an essay titled 'The "Touching" Effect', in which she said the touch of warm hands is necessary for the mental development of children.

While I read the work, I recollected the days when I was as young as the writer and devoted myself to bringing up my children.

In those days, as my two boys were dashing off to their primary school in the morning, I would say:

'Have you forgotten anything? You'll be late for school unless you hurry.'

They would answer back with the words 'I'm leaving home,' which is the Japanese usual address when leaving the house. I never failed to stop what I was doing and see them off at the front door. I would run after them and pat them on the head three times. Why three times? A Japanese proverb says, 'What happens twice will happen thrice', but my belief is that it will never happen four times. Boys are always very physical and may have accidents when out-of-doors. I felt, however, that patting my children three times had the effect of a charm that would drive away another repeated misfortune. After patting them three times, I would send them off, saying:

'Be careful on your way to school.'

I wonder how many years I repeated my charm 'ritual' every morning. When my eldest son got married, I asked a teacher who had been in charge of him in the fifth and sixth-year grades of primary school to give a speech at the wedding reception. To all the guests the teacher referred to my secret charm of patting my son and said:

'The bridegroom grew up enjoying his mother's tender feeling that this showed.'

I had no idea when my son wrote about my charm 'ritual' in his composition at school. When I read the young mother's essay, I felt like asking my children:

'Do you remember my charm ritual of patting you?'

'Of course. You ran after us even in your carpet slippers! How can we ever forget that?'

I am not sure what effect my customary charm ritual had on helping my children to grow up mentally. Still, it makes me happy that they remember their mother's silly morning ceremony.

TRANSLATED BY N. KUMABE

28.

What I Regret About Bringing Up My Children

Ayako Akutsu

****

I was taking a nap in a train, when I heard someone calling:

'Come here, Tecchan!'

Woken up by the voice, I saw a young mother who was standing close to me calling her son, who looked like a primary school pupil. His name, Tecchan, is the same name as my son's.

The boy in a grey shirt and chequered, short trousers came up and stood beside his mother. I said to myself:

'Oh, the boy looks so like my son in his childhood. Mischievous eyes in a round face! My son used to be like this.'

The marked tips of his fingers showed that they had touched many dirty things. Avoiding my gaze, he hid his hands. His sunburnt cheeks were quite rosy.

I used to be an office worker while my son was a little child. I used to get tired out from combining childcare and domestic chores without any help from my husband, and often felt so irritatable that I scolded my son in a loud voice. Looking at the boy in front of me, I said to myself:

'Why didn't I hug my son more tightly? He was so delightful!'

I reflected on how I had always forced him to be patient and behave himself as an elder brother to his younger sister. I should have encouraged him to get more affection from his parents, but just didn't have the energy to notice how attractive my son was. I was too concerned with my responsibility of bringing up my first child properly. I put too much emphasis on ensuring he became independent-minded. I constantly pushed myself in this regard.

Suddenly, I recalled a scene in the American film *Dad*, which I had seen a few years before. In the film an old couple fall ill one after the other. Their son in his forties, who lives far away from them, gives up his job and promptly goes to Los Angeles in order to look after them. It is the first time for the father and the son to face each other in earnest. Just before going into the operating theatre, the old father lifts himself up a little from the bed and hugs his son as if it were his last chance to do so.

'I never hugged you while you were a little child. I am very sorry for that now,' says the old man.

To hug his grown-up son – it is what he has left undone when he feels his time is drawing near. The grown-up son gently accepts his old father's hug. Jack Lemmon's splendid performance as the withered old father moved me to tears.

I shall never forget the film, which combines the glittering moments just before one's death with the glowing scarlet leaves of the autumn. In my own case, I may not have hugged my son enough, but I feel I have done my best in bringing him up. At least I am sure he appreciates my efforts. I am happy to see my son grown up as a gentle and mild man. It may be too late for me to act as Jack Lemmon did in the film – to make amends for what I should have done.

Tecchan, who is in front of me, is looking around with his curious eyes. When I look at his face, he seems embarrassed and looks down. That is so lovely.

TRANSLATED BY N. KUMABE

29.

My Daughter's Golden Hair – What a Waste!

Yoshiko Obata

****

The front door of our house was opened in high spirits. Mai, my daughter, jumped in, her golden hair also jumping up and down.

'Look! Look here! I was given this!' she said.

On her chest was hung a broach made from a slice of a zelkova tree with some words on it.

That night her school was engaged in community service activities in a summer festival of City F. All the students of the 11th year grade, which included my daughter, took part in the Yosa-koi dance, a well-known local dance of the community. The words on her broach said 'Yosa-koi, 2007'.

'They gave this to me because I danced so well. I was the only one to be given the award,' she said, proudly showing her wooden broach. Her golden hair was tangled with the white nylon string. She continued:

'Listen, Mum! A man in the festival committee said, "That was outstanding, delinquent!" when he hung this on me.'

She looked offended with her golden hair bundled with a rubber band. This style is exactly that of those juvenile delinquents who frequent Shibuya, one of the busiest parts of Tokyo. We see them so often on television that it was rather natural that the man called my daughter by that name. Thinking that way, I could not help smiling.

'Your golden hair and sunburnt face may make some people think that you are a delinquent,' I said, and my daughter expressed her discontent by pouting her lips, from which the lipstick had come off.

She spends all the holidays and her time after school involved in her club activities. She gets more and more sunburnt while she devotes herself to her outdoor exercise in the school grounds, especially in spring and summer. She stretched out her light brown arm and took a glass of iced tea, saying:

'Our high school does not impose any regulations on us. This freedom given to the students is special to our school. Still all the students behave sensibly.'

'That's what those involved say. But outsiders may not always see it in the same way,' I warned.

She looked straight at me with her pupils framed with dark eyeliner. Her manner was simply that of a sixteen-year-old girl. A grunt was her only answer. She looked up a bit. I could see bits of her dark hair through the little spaces of her golden hair braids. At the roots of her hair she had on some false hair called 'extensions'. She finished off a glass of iced barley water and said:

'As a matter of fact . . . adults regard hair colouring and make-up as the sign of a delinquent, don't they?'

'Yes, but only in the case of high school students,' I replied. Mai swelled her nostrils; the tip of her nose was decorated with pearls.

'That could well be true, but I can't understand it.'

'People in general make up their minds 90 % of the time according to what they see,' I said, although I knew she was not old enough to understand the absurdity of that observation.

My daughter, who was about to debate the point, picked up a strand of golden hair that had fallen on the table, using her nails varnished with floral patterns. I took the hair from her and threw it away into a wastepaper basket, saying:

'You, a high school student, still have a lot of growing up to do. Your body is still developing so that it will last on all your life. You should take good care of your skin and hair,' I said without hesitation.

But Mai, who has reached the awkward stage, immediately retorted:

'If you want to be beautiful in old age, you should take good care of your skin and hair while you are young.'

She became quite sulky. Seeing her made-up face still retaining some childish features, I continued to persuade:

'If you continue to dye your hair, it will harm both your skin and hair, and your hair will stop growing.'

She could not answer back, so I went on:

'Even the best dyes do not guarantee against the risk of going bald. And yet you continue to dye your hair?'

I picked up another golden hair from the table and showed it to her under her very eyes, saying mockingly:

'You wouldn't mind going bald? Ha-ha-ha!'

She immediately refuted my comments.

'I don't mind at all. If I went bald, I'd wear a wig. If you are right, all the golden-haired young men will end up wearing wigs. The time will come when everyone will wear a wig. That's just fine with me.'

At the moment when she raised her flat nose, her golden hair became entangled with her piercing. I wanted to say something more, but I noticed it was past midnight. I ended our talk by saying:

'It's time for you to take a bath. We shouldn't waste any more time.'

I thought we had once again wasted our time that night.

TRANSLATED BY N. KUMABE

30.

Dandelion

Kazuko F. Fujino

****

Twenty years ago, as a result of my husband's new assignment, we moved to a suburb of Kofu, 100 kilometres north-west of Tokyo. I often had to go out at that time for piano lessons, PTA meetings and other such commitments required by our four children, who were still young. With no other public transportation facilities I often used the Minobu line. It was a single-track railway with one or two trains every hour, usually one-car trains. In the daytime there were only a few passengers on the train.

Early one spring afternoon, I was hurrying home by train, which was nearly empty as usual. In contrast to the piercing chill outside, it was warm in the train, as if I were in a greenhouse. Seated nearby was a five- or six-year-old boy with a woman, presumably his mother. The boy twisted his body round in order to place his arms on the window frame and was gazing outside with his forehead pressed on the window pane. His mother whose make-up was pleasing enough sat next to him with her eyes closed, as if she was asleep.

The railway being a single-track line, the train stopped longer at some stations in order to let the trains coming in the other direction pass by. When the train stopped at one such station, the boy joyously yelled to his mother 'Mummy, mummy, look! Look at that! A dandelion!' He shook his mother's shoulder with his small hand. I followed the direction of his gaze. At the end of a rusted sidetrack covered with fallen leaves and probably no longer in use, there stood a bright yellow dandelion flower. Surrounding it was a desolate wintry scene. That spot alone appeared warm.

Somewhat abruptly, the mother said 'You are so noisy! What's the matter?' without turning towards the window, with her eyes closed.

She may have been thinking about something. She may have been just too tired to be bothered by the child's voice. The little boy, at a loss for a moment, stealthily drew back his hand, returned to his previous posture and went on gazing at the dandelion. The train set off again, as if nothing had happened.

After my own children grew up, I have often thought about that episode. That little boy may have felt the weight of his mother's burden and may have been making an effort as a child to please her. Whenever I remind myself of the image of the boy's small back as he observed the dandelion all by himself, a heart-rending emotion wells up within me.

I used to do the same thing as that mother. Now I know better. If she had simply said 'Oh, really?' and turned towards the dandelion, looked at it together with the boy, how relieved he would have been. What kind of other thought was left in the boy's mind, I wonder.

TRANSLATED BY THE AUTHOR

31.

My Son's Growth

Kumiko Miura

****

I have three children: my eldest daughter is in the second year of a postgraduate course, my eldest son is in the third year at university, and my second son is in the third year of senior high school.

I admit I am a restless and impatient person, and brought up my children in a less than calm atmosphere. This is most obvious in the case of my eldest son, two years younger than his sister and four years older than his brother. I'm afraid I neglected to recognize the different stages of his growth, although I know it is impossible to recognize every moment of a child's growth.

I do not remember the moment when he began to stand up or walk, whereas I do about his brother and sister. The fact is, I was rather amazed to find him toddling about in a room.

This is what happened before he was a year old. One day, he was playing in a sandpit with his sister at a park near our house. The next thing I knew was that he was sitting quietly with a smile at the top of a playground slide; he had been under the slide moments before. Since he was unable to walk at that time, he must have managed to crawl up the slide; he was so good at crawling. I still remember that I wondered how he could crawl up the slide and that I was very concerned that he might fall down.

The following is a story I still remember about a moment one autumn when he was five years old. It makes me think I was always watching his mental development. It is about a 'bell-ring' insect whose chirping only the Japanese have traditionally appreciated.

My eldest son was an active child fond of playing outside. Ya-kkun, U-chan and he, boys of the same age, living close to one another always played well when together. Ya-kkun and U-chan came to our house almost every day and called for my son in their loudest voices:

'Let's play outside, Nao-kun!'

One summer when they were five years old, the three boys were determined to catch insects. There was a river running in front of the apartment development area where we lived, and when the riverbed was dry you could always find a lot of insects such as locusts, praying mantises and ladybirds. U-chan was skilful enough to catch locusts with his hands and brave enough to run into the grass almost as tall as he was. Ya-kkun could even recognize a 'piggyback locust'. He had a good knowledge of insects' names and how to keep insects, under the influence of his elder brother, who was very keen on insects.

My eldest son was unable to catch an insect with his hands. Once he caught a migratory locust, but it felt so rough in his hands that he decided he didn't like it. While he ran after insects with his insect net, he sometimes put it over Ya-kkun's head, which made his friend very angry.

My son would take care of the insects he had caught, but he often let some of them die in an insect cage left at the entrance. I would say him:

'By all means, you may catch insects, but you had better let them go soon.'

I am not sure how much he accepted my advice.

One evening, we felt chilly in the gathering dusk of an autumn evening, when a friend of mine gave my eldest son a few 'bell-ring' insects. He immediately called his two friends and began taking care of the insects; they enjoyed putting pieces of eggplants and cucumbers in the cage and building a shelter with pieces of a flowerpot.

All my family listened to the insects' ringing chirp, and my eldest son took good care of them.

Then one day in late autumn, all the 'bell-ring' insects were not moving. The eldest son shook the cage, saying;

'The "bell-ring" insects aren't moving.'

I said, intending to comfort him:

'They are dead, but they must have laid eggs in the ground. I'm sure their baby insects will come out next year.'

His question was what I had least expected:

'Will the baby insects have no chance to see their parents?'

'Well . . . no, they won't,' was all I said.

At my words, he kept looking at the insects lying in the cage, while I silently watched him crouching by the cage. His limbs were rather broad, which resulted from his eating so much: he was not particular about food.

'I'll never ill-treat insects!' he declared very firmly. He must have learned something from 'bell-ring' insects at that early age.

'That's a good decision,' I said.

The transiency of autumn insects which must die soon, like the story of *Freddie the Leaf*, can never be understood by a little child. Nor can a small child understand the philosophy of 'life's rotation' that the end of a life is linked to the birth of another. Still, I felt happy at my son's open feelings and he became very dear to me.

As I recall that scene, I convince myself that it was a little moment in my son's mental development.

After that day, the three boys stopped catching insects and began enjoying building a tunnel in a sandpit.

TRANSLATED BY N. KUMABE

32.

A Phone Call at Midnight

Kazuko F. Fujino

****

I sensed some noise in the distance. Then, suddenly, it became a loud thundering noise that woke me up. The phone was ringing. My husband woke up to answer it, as I rushed to the extension in our living-room. Then the phone stopped ringing and remained silent. Who would call this early in the morning? They say there are telephones displaying caller ID. We don't have a modern phone with such a function.

We've had a series of hot summer days with a high during that day over 30 degrees Celsius. Did anything happen to my ageing mother-in-law or to my own father who is also getting old? A wall clock confirmed that it was a little after two in the morning. Should I phone them to confirm whether they called us? If my assumption was wrong, I would end up waking up their families. They are always putting the elder's needs first. If there is nothing important, they should be allowed to sleep through the night. If there was something critical, I am sure they would call again. For a while, I kept staring at the telephone while standing next to it. The telephone remained silent.

Then I started thinking about my four children living on their own away from us. The elder son, Takayuki, is not someone who would call us up when he is in trouble. After everything is settled, he would quietly report what had happened.

Could it be that either Megumi or Toshiyuki was in a traffic accident? She or he might have called us for help in vain, because we didn't answer the call, then she or he might have been running about trying to deal with the aftermath alone. I could easily picture the accident scene vividly. Wrecked cars, scattered pieces of windshield, injured people. They must be feeling helpless. Was that a life-threatening accident? Or did Megumi or Toshiyuki get injured and need help?

It must be daytime now in the US, where my eldest daughter lives. Did anything happen to Sakura my granddaughter? Although she might have dialled in a hurry for help, she would have realized there was no point in placing an emergency call over the Pacific Ocean in order to ask the help of parents living in Japan. She might just hang up and give up asking for help.

Only unpleasant events crossed my mind. It was only one phone call that I missed, and yet, I am so upset; how incompetent! I feel tight knots in my chest.

'Someone must have called the wrong number. Go back to sleep,' said my husband and closed his eyes.

It is summer. The day dawns early. Although it has not been long since I missed the call, it is getting lighter outside; I could see pale blue sky between the curtains. I opened the curtains in the living-room, then opened the glass doors. A chilly breeze came in, as if denying the fact that we had been experiencing consecutive hot summer days. The sky seems to be getting slightly lighter with buildings still in silhouette. It is a little too early for the birds to start chirping.

It is quiet. Right now, somewhere at this moment, there must be someone on their deathbed; someone must be being born. Somewhere in the world someone must have spent a horrifying day in a war zone crouching down under flying bullets. Someone might be hoping not to have another day of suffering in this life, someone might be so anxious to start another day to spread happiness. With all of its six billion crew on board bearing individual thoughts, the Earth keeps going steadily. How small and incompetent a human being is!

A long time ago, I recall it was while I was a student, I witnessed the dawn feeling how powerless one human being was. I was miserable and pitiful, and it was painful to recognize my stupidity and ugliness. How do we define true beauty? For what purpose was I born on this earth? What is my own mission, if there is one? Of course, I know I would never be able to find a concrete answer in my lifetime. It has been a while since I forced myself to examine who I am.

The phone did not ring again.

TRANSLATED BY THE AUTHOR

33.

After Ten Years

Yasuko Matsumoto

****

'How cold it is!'

'I hope it will be a white Christmas.'

We, a family of four, leave for my parent's house under the threatening sky. All of us carry parcels of gifts and a box of cakes in both hands. I do not know for certain when it started, but it is now our established custom to get together at my parent's house and have a party with my mother and my elder sister's family on Christmas Eve. My parent's house is so near. We have only to get off at the fourth railway station to get to it, but it is seldom that our family visit my mother, all together now that our children are fairly grown up.

I find my husband's younger sister's family also have come by car. We are fourteen altogether. The eldest boy, a university student, and other boys are all taller than five feet eight. It feels as if the house, which is actually large, has become smaller when the boys walk about in it.

Last year, everyone sat in a tight squeeze around the one large table in the dining-room, using all the extra stools. This year, we don't do that and the children sit around a low table in the living-room.

I hear each of the children in turn talk briefly about the big events they have experienced and about their hopes and plans for the coming year. My nephew, a third-year high-school student and the would-be master of ceremonies, has suggested the idea. I hear my sons talk normally, although they are reserved in speech at home. My nieces, who are talkative, interrupt the others. I hear laughter resounding around the children's table. There are already only a few pieces of broiled chicken left on the big dishes and very little salad left in the bowls.

When the children were small, we the parents prepared all sorts of activities to please them. We made them sing Christmas songs together with us and one of us played the part of Father Christmas.

'How big they all have grown!'

We the parents, who are sitting back around the dining table, express our surprise and joy at seeing our children grown up and happily drinking champagne and beer.

I recollect how I made my eldest son play together with my sister's two sons when they were small, for they were almost the same age. Especially when they were very small, my son being one or two years old, they were unable to understand what the parents wanted them to do, so it was for only a short time that the three of them played together on good terms in the same place. Soon they began to do whatever they liked individually. They scrambled for playthings. One got lost. Another began to cry because of tiredness. Taking care of the three was too much for my sister and me. We often asked my mother to help.

I had no time of my own. I was too busy to breathe, spending every minute of the day in taking care of them. I wished from the bottom of my heart that the children would grow up fast and leave us. Looking back now, however, I feel nostalgic about those old days. My heart sinks when I think those days will never come back.

'Look! Look! Over there!' Someone exclaims.

Hanging on the upper part of the living-room wall is a picture in a frame. It is a picture taken at the Christmas party just ten years ago. It was taken just after we exchanged gifts. My brother-in-law, who is dressed in the Father Christmas costume, sits in the middle of the children.

My eldest son, who was then in the third year of primary school, holds open the book he has just been given. He looks already absorbed in it. A university student now, he still likes reading books as much as he did ten years ago. My second son, who has broken into a broad smile, with big boxes of gifts under both arms, was then four years old. Now he is in the third year of junior high school. The naughty look in his eyes can be already seen in the ten-year-old picture. My nieces happily make the V sign. The youngest niece aged two fearfully looks up at Father Christmas.

All of them look so childlike and innocent as to make me laugh in spite of myself.

'Their bodies have grown bigger, but they remain somehow unchanged,' one of us says.

We the parents look satisfied at the picture with eyes half closed. I find some aspects of their personality already betrayed on their innocent faces.

'I've got a good idea! Let's take a picture of ourselves, sitting at the same place and in the same pose.' My nephew, the would-be master of ceremonies, proposes.

Each person sits at the same place and takes up the same pose as they did ten years ago. In place of Father Christmas, who is absent this year, my mother sits in the middle of the group. My elder sister and I tell them to pose, like they did in the original picture. 'Look at your gift with a happier expression!' 'No, no. Don't grin!'

'Let's take another picture like this in ten years' time,' says my nephew, when the photographing is over. We the parents incredulously stare back at him.

'You say so, but you will then say "I'll spend Christmas Eve with my sweetheart" or "Spending Christmas Eve with my parents is a boring idea" or something like that, won't you ?'

We surely know the children will soon leave us, but we the parents wish we will be able to get together with them again for another party like this in ten years' time.

TRANSLATED BY S. KURAMOCHI

35.

At an Antique Market

Junko Kawamura

****

In mid-December last year, I went to an antique market held in the International Forum square. When I arrived at the entrance at ten o'clock in the morning, a banner announcing 'O-edo Antique Fair' was billowing in the breeze. The square, surrounded by buildings on all sides, was mostly in the shade, with a few warm sunlit patches. There appeared to be as many as 150 stalls altogether.

The dozen-plus members of the antique appreciation circle that I belong to who had come along that day agreed to separate and meet up again in two hours.

Once on my own, I decided to make the rounds of all the stalls beginning at one end. The stalls started near Yurakucho Station and continued without a break all the way to Tokyo Station. It was crowded everywhere.

When the wind blew, yellow zelkova leaves fluttered to the ground, some landing on the goods for sale, adding a picturesque touch to the year-end antique fair atmosphere. Toys, glassware, pottery from Japan and abroad, books, daily commodities, used clothes, kitchen utensils, clocks and watches, cameras, accessories and junk – it was a veritable hodgepodge. At some stalls, goods were even placed directly on the ground.

I let my eyes roam over the goods on display. I wasn't looking for anything special that day, but if I found anything I liked, I'd be happy, I thought.

A small plate with a blue glaze design caught my eye. The light indigo blue colour of the cobalt oxide paint was superb, a little like the colour of the sky that day. Three blades of grass which looked like sweet galingales were painted on the white part in the centre. I asked the stallholder when the plate was made, and he answered, 'Edo, maybe?' That's anywhere from the seventeenth to the nineteenth centuries.

The stallholder told me the price was 23,000 yen for the set of five plates, but he added that he couldn't find the other four plates now. He didn't seem too eager to sell, so I gave up and decided to move on and look at the other stalls. Blue glaze plates were everywhere, but I didn't find any as attractive as that first small plate. Is this what they call love at first sight?

As time passed, the urge to find at least one thing to take home with me grew stronger, but as I went around the stalls, my thoughts kept going back to the small plate. I finally managed to find my way back to that particular stall.

'I really like the colour of this plate. Can't you sell me just this one?'

'Well, it's part of a set, you know.' He didn't seem to want to sell at all.

Even on hearing his reply, I couldn't give up the idea and kept admiring the plate in my hands. Then, in an apparent change of mind, the man said to me, 'It's true the colour of this cobalt oxide paint is beautiful. I may be able to sell them piece by piece . . .'

I jumped at this offer. 'Oh, good! I just want it for myself, so one is perfectly alright. I'll take it'.

The man sold me the plate for 4,500 yen, and I had it packed. I was so happy I felt as if a load had been taken off my shoulders. What a relief!

I later learned that this small plate is quite valuable. A member of our circle who is an antique shop owner looked at the plate and told me that it was old blue-and-white porcelain of the Tenkei era, made some time between the end of the Ming Dynasty and the beginning of the Qing dynasty, circa seventeenth century. It is old, and on top of that, it is porcelain from China. I have always been an impulsive shopper, and this was the first time I had bought anything prestigious with an authentic pedigree. I was proud of myself and thrilled.

I imagined what I would put on the plate. The green of cucumber, the yellow of pumpkin, the purple of eggplant, the orange of salmon and the white of tofu – all those colours would go well on the plate, making the sky-like indigo blue stand out even more.

Having acquired one item, I felt more relaxed and was strolling around when my eyes caught sight of a Susie Cooper flower pattern plate about 23 cm in diameter. It appeared to be a Dresden Spray. To my surprise, it was priced at 2,300 yen. It would normally cost six or seven times more. I looked at it carefully, thinking it might have some flaw, but it was in mint condition.

'Why is it so inexpensive?' I enquired.

'I got it cheap, that's why.'

I took out my wallet at once. I didn't ask for a discount, but the shopkeeper said, 'You can have it for 2,000 yen.' It was unbelievable. It is unexpected things like this that make antique markets such fun. I can't think of a more satisfying experience.

Susie Cooper is a British porcelain designer. Her pottery was also very popular in Japan a little while ago, and many young women were putting aside money as 'Susie Savings' to collect Susie Cooper tea sets and tableware. My daughter was very fond of her designs, too, so this will make a great present for her.

I like the unpretentious atmosphere of an antique market. I like the crowds and the stalls with their jumble of wares. I like it because sometimes you come across things that sparkle and stand out from all the other goods. I like it because you don't need a fat purse to enjoy it. You can have fun looking, buying and eventually using what you buy. An antique market is all these things for me.

TRANSLATED BY H. MIYAZAKI AND Y. TAKAHASHI

36.

With a Minor Flaw

Seiko Nakamura

****

The cup has dahlias drawn in fine cobalt blue lines on a creamy white base. From the flower, five vine-like stems stretch out all the way to the inside of the cup. The saucer has an onion depicted on it. From the onion, leaves are growing in three directions and small, pretty flowers are blooming at the tips of the leaves. The rims of both the cup and saucer are gently curved, with five small lumps between each curve.

This is none other than the world famous Meissen coffee cup, with the crossed swords trademark of Meissen on the underside. The most famous and representative Meissen pattern is, without doubt, the cobalt blue onion.

Rain was drizzling down that day in the middle of the rainy season. At tea-time, I took out the coffee cup from the cupboard with great care and was enjoying my coffee at leisure. The rain had made the leaves of the persimmon and camellia in the garden look greener. Was it because of the coffee cup that the coffee tasted much better than usual? I placed the cup gently on the table so as not to damage it. After all, it is one of the most expensive pieces of china in our house. The cup and saucer set cost 14,000 yen. And on top of that, I had bought it at the National Porcelain Company of Meissen itself, located in the eastern part of Germany.

When I was travelling through eastern Europe in early May, I saw the cup displayed at the Meissen company shop. To be precise, it was not in one of the lovely display cases but in a wagon of for-sale items. The tag attached to it said, 'with a minor flaw' in Japanese. I scrutinized it many times but could not find the flaw. I should have asked the shop assistant at the time, but it is too late now. It cost 3,000 yen less than the 'flawless' cup. That is to say, the cups in the display cases cost 17,000 yen. Why hadn't I paid 3,000 yen more and bought a 'flawless' cup?

In fact, I had set my mind on buying a coffee cup for myself in Meissen, but when the time came to actually make the purchase, I had wavered.

'It might break one day. It's only a coffee cup after all. Many cups that cost less are just as beautiful. After all, whatever cup I drink from, the coffee will taste the same,' I thought.

'No, no. I might never be able to come to this Meissen company again. Have I come all this way to go back without buying anything? Won't I regret it?'

These conflicting thoughts raced through my mind. The time to join the rest of the group was fast approaching. At that moment, I caught sight of the sales wagon, and it was in that wagon that I found this coffee cup 'with a minor flaw'. I snatched it up. Looking back now, I realize that the difference in price with the 'flawless' cup in the display case was only 3,000 yen, which may seem like a big difference to some, a small difference to others.

On top of it all, before my trip to eastern Europe, hadn't I proudly announced to almost everyone I met, 'I'm going to get a coffee cup in Meissen, a centrepiece of Hungarian embroidery in Budapest and a pair of Henckels scissors in Germany'? Despite all that, I feel angry at my stinginess which made me waver at the last moment. I went all the way there to end up buying a cup 'with a minor flaw'. It's laughable.

But I have a friend who went even further. Like me, she was saying excitedly that she was going to buy a coffee cup in Meissen, but when the time came, she said she would pass and she didn't buy anything at all in the end. I suppose such is human nature after all.

Thinking of all this, I finished my coffee. The cup on the table had such a dignified presence, exuding a flavour of European elegance, that it was hard to imagine it had 'a minor flaw'.

TRANSLATED BY H. MIYAZAKI AND Y. TAKAHASHI

37.

Cleaning Leaf Vegetables

Hatsuko Sakamoto

****

When cooking vegetables, the first thing you have to do is to clean the vegetable leaves. Unlike peeling onions or carrots, cleaning vegetable leaves is much harder for me, and it is a task I do not relish. I have a good reason for this.

I went to a Chinese restaurant with a friend many years ago. My friend ordered noodles with vegetables and meat, and I ordered ramen noodles. We both found the taste was not bad and were enjoying our noodles.

Until about half way through, I was busily eating to satisfy my hunger, but as my stomach settled down after a while, I began to eat at a slower pace.

When I eat noodles, I usually only pick up the noodles and don't eat the soup. I just sip a little soup with the soup spoon to taste it, so there is always a lot of soup left in my bowl.

It happened when I was almost finished. When I picked up some green spinach, I saw something white entangled with it. I immediately felt this was ominous and a chill ran down my spine. Holding the spinach between my chopsticks, I raised it to eye level and examined it carefully. What looked like a curly white elastic band which had gone a bit slack was the carcass of a creamy white insect, in fact, the length of half a little finger.

'You should show it to the proprietor.' My friend urged me repeatedly. She was really angry. I fully intended to do so and looked around the shop. Several customers were slurping up their noodles with relish. Somehow I hesitated to speak up.

'If you aren't going to say anything, I'll make the complaint for you,' my indignant friend kept saying, but I dragged her along and left the shop.

My stomach was not content either. I might have imagined it, but that night I felt a stinging pain in the stomach. I thought I should have at least told the proprietor in private.

I couldn't eat Chinese cuisine for quite a while after that, and ever since then, I have become very meticulous about cleaning leaf vegetables.

This is how I do it. I put on my reading glasses and wash each leaf very carefully in a bowl, changing the water many times. I rub and squeeze each leaf by hand. I then put the leaf vegetable under the tap and wash it under running water. When I have finished, the leaf vegetables have a wilted look, and the once fresh thick green leaves are all thin and transparent. When I clean cabbage leaves, for example, I have to wash each leaf, carefully examining both sides of the leaf, so it takes a long time. By the time I am finished, most leaf vegetables have shrunk so much in size that they don't need any cutting.

Anyway, it is a very exhausting job for me. But as I like vegetables more than anything else, I continue to busily wash away so I can eat them at ease.

TRANSLATED BY H. MIYAZAKI AND Y. TAKAHASHI

38.

A Bed and Breakfast in Sweden

Setsuko Terao

****

I found a lace doily all crumpled up in the corner of a drawer when I was sorting things out. The doily, about 20 centimetres in diameter, was handmade and the lace stitches of the intricate pattern were deftly done. I waved it at my husband.

'I'd forgotten I had put it here. Do you remember this?'

'Yes. Isn't it the one we got at the B&B in Sweden?' My husband sounded nostalgic.

My thoughts went back to that day almost forty years ago when we were living in Germany. We took a family trip around the Scandinavian countries in early September. After driving around Finland, we crossed to Stockholm by ferry. After some sightseeing, we headed for Oslo in our car. Oslo is about 600 kilometres due west of Stockholm, and it was not a motorway, so the distance was too long for a day's drive. On top of that, we started out late which meant that we had to find somewhere to spend the night along the way.

We hadn't seen many people around town even in Stockholm, and when we left the city, we hardly saw any cars or people. Only the road stretched straight westwards on and on through the forest. The leaves were beginning to change colour, and though it was still early September, it was already slightly chilly and the grass along the road looked brownish.

We would be in trouble if it got dark on a road like this where you had to drive for miles before passing another car. We were speeding along, slightly worried, when we finally spotted what appeared to be a village. In small towns and villages, bars or pubs often have rooms upstairs and offer bed and breakfast, so we drove slowly looking for a sign.

We stopped the car at a wooden building that seemed to be what we were looking for. When I went in and asked, I was told we could have a room upstairs, just as I had expected. It appeared to be a pub, with a few customers sitting on stools drinking and munching on snacks.

When we entered the pub with our two pre-school-age boys, everyone looked at us with a look of surprise. It was apparently extremely rare to see Asian children around at the time, so we got used to the boys being the centre of attention everywhere we went. We had dinner there, went up to our room to put the children to bed and came down again to ask about breakfast the next morning.

The pub was already closed, and the middle-aged landlord and his wife were relaxing in their living-room in the back. When we went in, a huge bulldog sitting comfortably in the armchair moved his eyes in our direction. In Europe, we were always impressed by how well the dogs are trained and how well the children are disciplined. Some dogs slowly approached us to sniff us from time to time, but I seldom heard them bark.

'Are you Chinese or Japanese?' the landlord asked. When we replied that we were Japanese, he seemed somewhat pleased. 'A few years ago, there was a car accident in this village and a Japanese man was injured and stayed here for about half a year. He was a very nice person.'

His wife took out a large guestbook and showed it to us. The man had written in English that he was very grateful for the kindness that was shown him here after the accident. This must be why this couple has a special affinity for the Japanese.

'Actually, we want to leave very early tomorrow morning, but will you be up?'

'We won't be able to serve you breakfast at six.'

'Then, we would like to pay for our room now.'

We had spent all the Swedish money we had for dinner that night, so we offered them German marks. The landlord's wife took it and held it up as if to see through it. 'I've never seen German money.'

We were surprised that they had never seen German marks when in this area German is better understood than English.

The couple turned the bill this way and that, discussing the current exchange rate. We volunteered some information, telling them how much the exchange rate was in the hotel in Stockholm, but they still continued to look perplexed. If we wait for the bank to open the next morning, we won't be able to reach Oslo before nightfall. We were at a loss what to do when the landlord came up with a suggestion. 'I've never seen German money so I can't accept it, but don't you have something Japanese?'

During our trip, we cooked rice whenever we stayed in places where we could cook for ourselves so we had rice bowls, chopsticks and also lacquer soup bowls in the car. We brought them from the car and displayed them. The couple seemed to take a liking to the pattern on the lacquer soup bowls and picked up the bowl and a pair of chopsticks. 'We'll accept these as payment for your board. We'd also like to give you something as a memento.' He took out a lace doily from the cupboard nearby and gave it to us.

We started out early the next morning. After we drove through the still slumbering village, we realized we had left a jacket in the room and went back. When we went in again, no one was up yet so we retrieved the jacket and continued our journey.

True, we had only used the bedroom and left without breakfast, but we had stayed the night for almost nothing, and the landlord of the small bed & breakfast had even given us a souvenir. I wonder where that village actually was. The blue lace doily the colour of forget-me-nots stirred up old memories and we sat there for a while quietly reminiscing.

TRANSLATED BY H. MIYAZAKI AND Y. TAKAHASHI

39.

The First Grade Bowl of Rice with Chicken and Eggs

Asako Ono

****

I went shopping with my father on 27 December, only a few days before the end of the year. When we finished our business, it was a little too early for lunch, but my father suggested that we should have 'Oyako-Donburi', a bowl of rice with chicken and eggs, at 'Tamahide', a Japanese restaurant of long standing, at Nin-gyo-cho, one of the busiest parts in Tokyo.

We ordered our food and paid for it at the counter in front of the reception room. The most popular menu there was 'The Original Oyako-Donburi', (¥1,300) but we ordered 'The First Grade Oyako-Donburi' (¥1,500).

A lady sitting at the counter in a kimono, repeatedly asked about the difference between 'The Original' and 'The First Grade', answered coolly without showing any emotion:

'In "The First Grade", rice is topped by soft-boiled eggs with soup, while in "The Original", rice is topped by hard-boiled eggs, in an old-fashioned way.'

We weren't kept waiting long before we were served the first menu of chicken-bone soup. Its nice taste satisfied my thirst while waiting for the main course.

The bowl of rice soon succeeded the soup. I immediately opened the lid. The rice served flat in the bowl was topped by well cooked eggs with onions and chicken. The other customers in the same room were having 'The Original' with hard-boiled eggs. The topping of 'The First Grade' had not only half-done eggs but also a small raw egg in the middle, just like a full moon. The chicken, which played a leading part, was softer than I had expected, and had no offensive smell at all. Every time I have 'Oyako-Donburi', I am involved in some intricate thoughts about the name: 'Donburi' is plainly a bowl and 'Oyako' means parent and child, so the name of 'Oyako', or parent and child, was given to signify the coalescing of a chicken and its egg.

The salted and sweetened soup spread over rice tastes exquisite and never hinders the melting feeling of eggs. 'The First Grade Oyako-Donburi' is so juicy as a whole that we have it using its own spoon, not chopsticks. The black-lacquered spoon looked very substantial, but I examined it and found it was made of plastic. Since I had never visited the restaurant 'Tamahide', I asked my father if the food served there always tasted the same.

'It always tastes the same. "The First Grade Oyako-Donburi" is cooked by the chef himself who is preceded by seven masters,' said my father.

That may be the reason why 'The First Grade' is higher in price. Some may consider ¥1,500 too expensive while others may think it moderate. Anyway, I believe 'The First Grade Oyako-Donburi' is superb and you should never have it in any place other than 'Tamahide'.

TRANSLATED BY N. KUMABE

40.

Longing for Eggs

Keiichi Kawasaki

****

I love eggs. I can eat any number of eggs every day for every meal. I can't count the number of times I vowed never to touch alcohol again after suffering from a dreadful hangover the day after a heavy drinking spree, but I have never felt I don't want to see another egg even after gorging myself on eggs.

At a conveyor belt sushi bar, I always go first for the plate with a thick over-sized Japanese omelette sitting on sushi rice, and while I'm still eating it, I am already looking around to see when the next thick omelette sushi will be coming my way.

When I was at primary school, thinly shredded omelette was part of the standard menu of my lunch box I took to school. Sometimes it was spread over salty-sweet mince and pickled ginger to make a tricolour lunch box. Sometimes thinly sliced snow peas, yet another colour, was added to this to make a scenic tricolour lunch box.

I love regular omelettes, too. I love nothing more than putting a drop or two of Worcester sauce onto the half-cooked soft part inside the omelette and slurping it up. It's heaven itself for me.

Then, there's cracking open an egg and pouring it onto just-cooked hot rice. . . . Well, I can go on forever, but anyway, even if a scantily dressed beauty approached me hand in hand with an egg, I swear my eyes would not waver from the egg.

But alas, with just one word from my doctor, a restriction has been placed on my consumption of eggs, eggs that I love and pine for every day and night.

'Father, only one egg a day for you.'

Our family doctor, seated in front of me at the hospital, is our daughter's husband. Since I had my gallbladder removed, I am ordered to take a blood test from time to time. He says I don't have to take any medicine yet, but my total cholesterol level is too high or whatever; hence, the golden rule.

I have no way out because my wife, who has complete faith in our family doctor, accepts this golden rule as Gospel truth and follows it to the letter. Saying that if she fries or scrambles an egg, it becomes a mere lump, and I wouldn't know where it went in and merely crave for more, she's taken to serving a boiled egg for breakfast these days. That's it, nothing more. Until dawn breaks to usher in another day, no more eggs for me. It is pure agony.

When I was having dinner with our daughter's family one day, I fortified myself with a drink or two of beer and said to our family doctor, with slight rancour showing in my voice. 'Only one egg a day. I'm keeping your rules.'

The doctor, who had been informed of my discontent by my wife, instantly guessed what I was getting at and chuckled. 'Well, you know, you can have up to two. But then, the next day, you can't have any.'

'Oh, is that how it works?'

'Yes, but you can't have three even if you go without any for the next two days.'

These days I sometimes wonder. When will I be able to eat as many eggs as I want without any reproach or rebuke?

One day, when my end is near, will my wife place a plate full of thinly shredded omelettes of different flavours, savoury, sweet and soy sauce, in front of me and say, 'Dear, it's alright now. You can eat as much as you like,' holding back her tears? No, I wouldn't like that!

Even if it is a month before my last day, it will still be a tearful meal.

If it is five years before my last day, it might be better, but if I eat the eggs, will it mean the five-year lifespan will shorten by a year?

How about taking the middle course and making it a year before my last day? Is that an acceptable compromise? Even if my lifespan is shortened, it will only be a matter of months. But then, who is to decide my last day? No, this won't work either.

Longing for Eggs

A plate piled high with thinly shredded omelette, regular omelettes and thick Japanese omelettes, raw eggs on steaming rice. The day I can stuff myself with all these eggs will probably never come. However hard I try, I cannot stop the flow of time nor can I know when my life is coming to an end. All I can do is go on stoically and nobly with my life, carrying the burden of the golden rule on my shoulders. For myself and for my beloved wife, on New Year's Day or Christmas Day, whether it shines or rains, there is only one egg a day for me.

TRANSLATED BY H. MIYAZAKI AND Y. TAKAHASHI

41.

As If I Were in Paradise

Asako Ono

****

My sixteen-year-old daughter loves taking a bath like most Japanese do. As a little baby with her head wobbly, she did not mind water or shampoo getting into her eyes. Even when she was one or two years old, she often asked for a bath in the evening at the house where she was staying as a guest. She would lisp out audaciously:

'Get a bath ready for me.'

When she travelled to a hot spring, as soon as she was in the warm water of the bathhouse, she would say like an old woman:

'I feel so happy I could be in Paradise.'

The others in the bath looked at her in surprise. Anyway, as far as I remember, she never grizzled in the bath during her infancy.

My parents' house is an old one made of wood, and the bathroom is at the far end. On entering the bathroom, you find yourself in a small dressing-room, beyond which is a large washing area covered with draining boards. The wooden bath-tub, with the fragrance of a Japanese cypress, is deep, and children have difficulty in climbing over the brim.

When I visited my parents' home after I got married, my mother was afraid that the time-worn bathroom might be shunned by her granddaughter. She got together a toy duck, a watering pot and a water pistol and put them in the washing area to please her little grandchild. This caused my daughter's liking for a bath to change to loving a long bath.

For years when my family lived in my husband's company flat, he dreamed of getting out of the small apartment, but he was always scrupulous about choosing a comfortable bathroom.

The house where he was brought up was much larger than my parents' house, but he always seemed to be dissatisfied with its small bath-tub. When the house was rebuilt, he made a special request regarding the bathroom. He requested that the new bathroom should have large windows, a large washing area and a big bath-tub where they could lie with their legs extended. He stated that he would make no concessions as far as that was concerned although he knew that the space for the bathroom was rather limited. After the rebuilding was finished, he naturally took charge of cleaning the bathroom. Even now he does a perfect job of cleaning the bath-tub and the washing area of our house.

We moved to our new house one spring when my daughter was in the fourth year of primary school. While we lived in my husband's company flat, she did not mind having a bath with her father, but when taking a bath in the large bathroom of the new house, she insisted on taking it alone. My husband looked a little lonely.

As a junior hugh school pupil, my daughter began to wear her hair long. Naturally she spent more time in shampooing and hair treatment. She took more care of washing her face in order to deal with the problem of her teenage spots. She would stay in the bathroom for at least half an hour.

As a senior high school pupil, she came to spend even more time in the bath. She took a waterproof CD player with her into the bathroom, where she stayed until she had finished listening to one album. Almost every day she quarrelled with my husband, who stood just outside the bathroom and told her to come out at once. When she remained there for over an hour, I called out to her:

'You'll have a rush of blood to the head! Come out at once!'

She pays little attention to her parents' anxiety and irritation. She continues to sing with the shower-head in her hand as if it were a microphone.

When our new house was completed, we could not afford to put aside a special budget for future improvements to the house. The bathroom, which was of the latest style, is now seven years old, and we often talk of updating it; we think of introducing a jet bath, or, for example, equipping it with a hot-air drier.

Once when we were on holiday I went shopping with my husband and visited a showroom of N Company. There is now much focus given to ecology matters, and a bathroom with the latest improvements includes the use of hot water in a variety of ways.

I was attracted by a 'hot-air drier for a bathroom with mist functions of warm water'. It sprays water a little warmer than body temperature from the wall around the room. When you are sprayed you sweat and eliminate waste matter, your body getting renewed in this way. The machine also helps to get rid of stress. My husband was fascinated by a bath system with a bathtub you can automatically clean just by pushing a button. The television in the bathroom has a liquid crystal screen as big as that of a personal computer. Its waterproof remote-control which floats in the bathtub operates both the television and the hot water supply system. They also displayed a bathroom whose ceiling is coated with special paint to look like a night sky and is changed into a planetarium by pressing a switch to change the light.

Many of the devices exhibited there could be bought for about two hundred thousand yen and interested me a lot. I thought it was lucky for me not to be with my daughter at the time. If she had been there, she would have asked us to buy some of these items!

TRANSLATED BY N. KUMABE

42.

Today Is a Lucky Day

Yoko Usuda

****

Early one Sunday morning, when I had decided to sleep in, my husband called to me. He had woken up early and said, 'It's a beautiful day. Let's go for a walk in Musashiseki Park.' Although I wanted to lie in bed a little longer, I thought that it wouldn't be such a bad thing to walk beneath the trees in bloom and jumped out of bed. We had a quick breakfast and set off.

We walked a little bit slower than usual while we enjoyed the surroundings and arrived at the park. My husband, who has become very fond of digital cameras, took a small one that day and carried it in his hand.

We walked almost completely around the pond, and then came across a group of people. About twelve or thirteen Sunday cameramen were waiting for something with their big telephoto lenses which seemed to have a 20-centimetre radius. They were all standing in a line.

These are the kingfisher-watchers that I have heard about. I heard from someone that every week there are many amateur cameramen who try to photograph a kingfisher. They take positions around the pond and wait.

Moving my eyes from the cameramen to the surface of the pond, someone said 'Oh, a kingfisher!!!' There was the bird flying by with such a beautiful blue colour on its back. It landed on a small twig that was sticking up out of the water. There was a voiceless hubbub. Suddenly, there was the sound of many camera shutters clicking at the same time. I looked at my husband: he was also adjusting his camera in a hurry.

'I got it!!!'

That is the good thing about a digital camera. We can see the picture that we take straight away. The rippling of the water, the dried twig protruding from it, and the kingfisher were all in the picture. It was great timing. It made us feel a little bit sorry for those people who had been waiting for the chance for days and days.

'We were lucky today.' Without thinking we both said it at the same time.

TRANSLATED BY P. HALTMAN

43.

An Evening at the Kabuki

Chizuko Bando

****

The Kabuki-za theatre is a ten-minute walk from the underground station along Ginza street. The street was quieter and more relaxed than usual that day, the second day of the three-day weekend in February. The Kabuki-za, with its classic appearance, has a 120 year history but the current theatre was actually rebuilt in 1951. I am told that another rebuilding plan is in the offing as the current building is getting quite old.

It is the 'Matsumoto Hakuo 27th anniversary memorial performance' at the Kabuki-za this month, with programmes consisting mainly of plays which were Hakuo's favourites, played by actors who are closely related to the late Hakuo in one way or another.

'Matsumoto Hakuo', formerly called 'Koshiro', was well known as an actor with a presence, an actor of high calibre, a representative actor of his times. The current 'Koshiro' who succeeded to his name is his son, who used to be called 'Somegoro'. The son of 'Kosihro' is now called 'Somegoro'. The names 'Hakuo', 'Koshiro' and 'Somegoro', passed on from father to son, are eloquent testimonials to the hereditary family structure which is the backbone of the kabuki world.

A son born to one of the great kabuki families is trained in dance and song from a very young age. He learns from watching his father and starts acting on the stage even as a child. It is in this way that the tradition of kabuki has been preserved and continued over the years.

As it is a special performance today, five actors closely related to the late Hakuo – his two sons, his grandson and two other relatives – welcomed the audience by lining up on the stage during the interval, dressed in traditional formal attire, consisting of a stiff sleeveless jacket and a long, pleated skirt. They recounted episodes from the life of the late Hakuo, including some humorous ones that aroused laughter from the audience, another manifestation of kabuki being very much a family business.

The word 'kabuki' derives from the word 'kabuku', a word which describes someone who acts or dresses unconventionally, unlike anyone else. A kabuki play, which presents a dramatic story using exaggerated gestures and lines, flourished as a popular entertainment for the common folk in the Edo period – from the seventeenth to nineteenth centuries. Loyalty as the mainstay of the ideal samurai, or the emotional ties between parent and child, between brothers, or between lovers, were intertwined and dramatized to evoke laughter or move the audience to tears.

In spite of those beginnings, kabuki is often considered 'inaccessible and difficult' today. When I first started going to kabuki, I, too, felt it strange that heavily made-up male actors were speaking in female voices. In particular, I could not bring myself to like the exaggerated gestures of the actors and the growling *gidayu* chant, but I was soon overwhelmed by the colourful costumes and the beautiful colour schemes of the stage settings. In the dance plays, the stage takes on an even more ethereal quality, for a short while making you forget the mundane world and enjoy yourself in a world of dreams.

My seat that day was at the centre of the first row on the first floor balcony, so I had a full view of the stage. On my left were two elderly ladies sitting in a relaxed mood. On my right, my husband seemed very pleased with his rented audio-guide. This audio-guide is a great idea, carefully guiding the uninitiated through the world of kabuki. You first pay 650 yen plus a deposit of 1000 yen, which you get back when you return the audio-guide. There is an English version, too.

A special treat at the Kabuki-za is the theatre lunch box which you can enjoy in your seat during the intermission, a pleasure I look forward to each time. I think it must be a remnant of the times when kabuki was played in humble playhouses hundreds of years ago. Soon after our appetites were satisfied, the next play, *The Revenge of the Soga Brothers*, began.

The play is performed keeping time with music. Kabuki is made up of three elements, music (*ka*), dance (*bu*) and acting (*ki*). As background music, the shamisen, a three-stringed instrument, drum and flute are also essential elements as well as the chanting of the *gidayu* and *nagauta*, the long epic songs.

The last play of the day was a dance play in which Somegoro appeared as a high-ranking lady-in-waiting. He was both elegant and beautiful. In the second part of the play, the lady-in-waiting played by Somegoro is possessed by the spirit of a lion and dances in a frenzy, tossing about his long white mane. This was even more spectacular than the first part of the play. The pair of butterflies that taunt the lion, played by child kabuki actors, were also warmly applauded for their sweet and lively dance. We spent more than four delightful hours in this way, totally divorced from everyday life. After the performance, all of us left the Kabuki-za theatre, flushed with excitement, with an indescribable sense of uplift and elation.

Kabuki is well-known as Japan's traditional performing art with a history of more than three centuries. Besides carrying on this tradition, the young actors are now trying hard to bring in new trends by engaging in various outside activities. That is all the more reason why I wish to continue to keep in close touch with kabuki in the years ahead.

TRANSLATED BY H. MIYAZAKI AND Y. TAKAHASHI

44.

A Little Leading Actor

Kiyoko Nakajima

****

My husband and son are performers of *nagauta* music, a long epic song performed as the background music of the kabuki. They sometimes appear on the stage of a kabuki performance and I often go to the theatre.

These days, when I see a play in which little children are taking an active part, I am easily moved to tears and take out a handkerchief from my bag as I sit in the darkness. That may be because I am so advanced in years.

This is what happened while I was watching the staging of 'Shigenoi Parting from Her Child' at a seat in the back row of the Kabuki-za theatre. The play was nearing the end. Shegenoi, the mother, had lived separately from her little son Sankichi for a number of reasons. They had had no news of each other until she met her son, who was now a packhorse driver. They introduced themselves to each other. The young helpless son clung to his mother, who had married a samurai, a Japanese warrior. Shigenoi, however, repressed her motherly love and thrust Sankichi away with the dignity and courage befitting a member of a samurai family.

I had held back my heartbreaking grief and withheld tears, but I could not control myself any longer. The moment Sankichi began to sing the packhorse driver's song after being pushed away, my lachrymal glands loosened and tears overflowed onto my lashes.

It was just at that moment that I heard a little child's voice coming from the seat in front of me:

'Pee-pee!'

Turning my eyes dim with tears in that direction, I saw a boy aged four or five years old leaving his seat and walking to the door at the back of the theatre. A woman in Japanese dress who seemed to be his mother stood up in a fluster and followed him, saying:

'Sh! Be quiet! Hush! Hush!'

In the theatre the audience in their seats were calling the actors by their hereditary stage titles. On the stage, Sankichi was slowly leaving, crying and turning back to his mother again and again. When he disappeared completely, the curtain fell amid a thunderous clapping of hands. I had had my attention diverted by the child, but at the finale of the play I clapped my hands as ardently as any other member of the audience.

When I come to think of the kabuki performance, I find that child actors are given an important part, and I have a great admiration for them. They perform on the big stage of the Kabuki-za theatre at an early age together with adult actors. They must sometimes play a difficult role like that of Sankichi and even sing the pack-horse driver's song. They start their acting career at the age of four or five, and continue to work hard all through the consecutive twenty-five days of the performance, never absent from it due to illness, even on rainy or windy days. They must have many hard days of rehearsal before the premiere.

The hall gradually became light. I looked around and found people standing up with their eyes deep-red. They must have been moved by the splendid plot of the play and by the excellent performance of Sankichi.

The little actor will have a lot of trials and experiences amid the everyday applause. In this way he will inherit his father's fame and grow up to be an excellent actor. When he is convinced that he has done his best, he will applaud himself, and this will help him add to his confidence and courage. With this thought in mind, I said to myself:

'That little actor's performance will be a great hit every day.'

Feeling the after-effect of great admiration, I went out into the lobby. In a corner near the crowded toilets, I found a young mother in Japanese dress and her little son in his kindergarten uniform standing side by side. I remembered seeing them at a dressing-room when my husband performed at the Kabuki-za theatre, though I had no idea when it was. They must have been an actor's wife and child.

After exchanging greetings, I passed in front of them, when I suddenly became aware that it was this child who had cried, 'Pee-pee!' I assumed he had come to cheer his fellow actor who played the part of Sankichi, or he might have come for study purposes. I said to him in my mind:

'You've been working hard, I know. Stick with it!'

The child yawned a big long yawn, holding his mother by the hand. The mother said nothing, but watched him with a smile.

I felt relieved at the sight. As a matter of fact, my grandchild made his debut on the stage at the age of three as the third successor of a *nagauta* music performer.

Japanese traditional art is taught from generation to generation, and children are trained even at an early stage of life.

When I went out of the Kabuki-za theatre, I was greeted by the setting sun shining dazzlingly.

TRANSLATED BY N. KUMABE

PART 6

THOSE DAYS IN BRITAIN

45.

Remembering London in Those Days

Sachiko Mibu

****

'2 Mary Adelaide Close'. That was our address in London for four and a half years, when we were living there more than twenty years ago.

I arrived at Heathrow Airport early one morning in September 1980, with our baby son, who had just turned one year old. My husband had already been in London for three months by then. I looked around for him but he was nowhere in sight. When he finally arrived, still half asleep, with his hair all tousled, we had been kept waiting for over half an hour. As soon as he picked up his son, the baby wailed with all his might. That was the rather inauspicious beginning of our life in London.

Pulling ourselves together, we got into the car and arrived at a small but cozy, pleasant-looking house. It more or less satisfied my hopes. I had asked for a house that did not have to have the stateliness of a typical English house but a new, bright-looking house with plenty of running hot water at all times. The house had a living/dining-room and a kitchen on the ground floor, three bedrooms on the first floor, and even a small garden at the back. It was a compact, well-built house intended for young families such as ours. When my anger at being made to wait at the airport had finally subsided, my husband proudly showed me the car he had already bought for my use.

I soon found out why he was so well-prepared. Our house was in the middle of nowhere with no stations nearby and it was impossible to move about without a car.

The house was near Wimbledon, a familiar name to Japanese people. For my husband, who worked for an airline company, its location, being thirty minutes by car both from the office in town and from the airport, seemed to have been the decisive factor in making the choice.

I soon found out another reason for the prompt purchase of my car. My husband was so busy that he had no time at all to look after his wife and child. From the day after our arrival, the only thing I could count on was this car. With a map in one hand and a Japanese friend who had arrived in London a little earlier acting as my guide and telling me where to do the shopping, I had to somehow manage to get about on my own.

In those days, we were told in Japan that small children should be taken outdoors for fresh air as much as possible, but in London, the sky was often overcast and sunny days were few and far between. Whether I was doing the dishes or having a meal, whenever there was a little sunshine, I would quickly put the baby in the pram and hurry to nearby Richmond Park, but I didn't see many mothers with their children. I was told that there weren't many outdoor play areas in the park because most houses had gardens for the children to play in. I also heard that it was only the needy who came to the park, and my enthusiasm for the park was quickly dampened.

When we had more or less settled down and our daily routine was established, we were faced with the task of inviting back, one after another, my husband's colleagues and superiors who had had him over for meals when he was a temporary bachelor. This involved going out shopping, cleaning the house and cooking dinner for the guests. Early evening was when the baby tended to make a fuss and start crying. The small living-room would still be in a mess, cluttered with toys all over the place when it was time for the guests to arrive any minute. I felt like crying myself. Both the baby and I ended up in a state of near panic.

'Do you think we need to invite them all back? We do have a small baby after all,' I grumbled and often quarrelled with my husband, who is a stickler for fulfilling one's social obligations.

The season soon changed from autumn to winter. The cold weather was depressing, but what was more depressing was that it already became dark at about three o'clock in the afternoon. International calls were not as inexpensive then as they are now, and the internet and e-mail did not exist. I often wrote to my parents and my sister to complain about this and that. I would write lengthy letters saying, please send me this, the life here is very inconvenient as they don't have that, and so on. My sister wrote back in response one day, 'Why don't you try to do your best with the things you have there?'

Those words jolted me awake. 'That's right. I'd better make the most of living in London now. I'm going to have fun!'

I decided to put my complaints behind me and move on. I was now able to drive anywhere on my own, had found a good babysitter and had friends that I got along with. I must make the most of the few years we were going to be in London and enjoy myself. It had taken me about six months to feel that way.

We had another baby boy two years later and time went by quickly. It was common for Japanese expatriates to have to relocate several times during their posting in those days to suit the landlord's convenience or for other reasons. But fortunately, we were able to live in our first house the whole time we were in London. I became friends with a Lebanese woman called Hala living on the same street and our families became very close. The night before we left for Japan, Hala arranged for us stay over at her house and we bade each other a fond farewell. I still cherish the memory of that evening.

'2 Mary Adelaide Close'. I feel that we really started functioning as a family in that house.

We had been married for three years when we were transferred to London. Prior to that, we had lived near my parents' house in Tokyo and often spent our weekends having fun with friends from our school days. My husband was in sales and he spent most of his time talking to people around his age. His work seemed to me like a continuation of campus life.

But all this changed in London. We were suddenly on our own as a family. My husband was really very busy. One of his duties was to attend to the VIPs on their arrival at the airport. At the time, the flights from Japan arrived very early in the morning, and on top of that, they often arrived earlier than scheduled due to the trade winds. After entertaining clients at night, my husband would come home past midnight and check on the next morning's flight by phone. I remember him often sighing and saying, 'The plane is arriving at five again tomorrow.'

During the four and half years in London, my husband says he went to the airport nearly 400 times. The only time he was late was when he came to meet us, his wife and child; the episode has now become a family joke.

'I was greatly relieved when you came to meet me as soon as the plane landed.' He says many people have thanked him with these words wherever he went, even many years after his return to Japan. My husband, who was then a junior employee, was given the chance to meet many top leaders of Japanese companies that he would not otherwise have met. This has been a great asset in his later career.

I now realize that I, too, gained confidence in myself as a wife and mother thanks to the life in London, where I had to drive around on my own through unknown streets, negotiate with the repair man or consult the doctor in English by myself.

When I revisited London five years ago, I went to look at this house filled with many fond memories. As it is a brick house, the appearance had not changed that much except that there was perhaps somewhat more ivy crawling along the wall.

No one from those days including Hala, was living there anymore. I was surprised that I did not feel any emotion at the sight of the house. It was probably because my husband and children were not there with me. I thought then that I would like to come and visit the house again with my family, with whom I can share the memories of those days.

TRANSLATED BY H. MIYAZAKI AND Y. TAKAHASHI

46.

No. 81 The Chase

Fumi Ishii

****

'The trip was really very pleasant! Whenever I think of it, it makes my heart flutter.'

This is a fax from Ms K, a fellow member of our essay group. It is nearly a month since the two of us walked, like ones possessed, on that large common covered in greenery in June. The scene returns to my mind several times every day.

It was the last day of our eight-day trip to England and it was a day of free time. In the morning, two of us and another tourist paid a visit to the Tower of London reminding ourselves of Natsume Soseki's novel *London Tower*. After this we had lunch at a pub which Sherlock Holmes used to favour. Since Ms K. and I had our own plans, we left the other friend at the pub.

Ms K and I had wanted to visit the Natsume Soseki Museum even before we left Japan, but in London what had been causing us some anxiety became reality. All the people around us were, of course, foreigners. We had to use the Underground, but could we make ourselves understood in English? Could we manage to get to our destination, using poor English? But our desire to carry out our plan without missing this opportunity was stronger than our anxiety.

The name of the Underground station was Clapham Common, and the address was '81 The Chase'. I knew those two names because I had telephoned the Japan Tourist Bureau before the trip and learned them together with the necessary information about where the Soseki Museum was and how to get there. I repeated those names in my mind as if I were chanting a spell.

I took the Northern Line on the Underground. Despite some unexpected trouble with carriage doors, I managed to change trains and reached Clapham Common in almost an hour. On leaving the station, I found myself in a busy street, where I asked a passer-by:

'Excuse me. Could you help me?'

When I mentioned 'Soseki Museum', he inclined his head as if in doubt.

'What is Soseki?'

Another passer-by told me the way there. After I had walked for a while, I felt so anxious that I asked someone else in order to make sure of the way. This person went into his house to get a map. To my surprise, I found we were walking in the opposite direction.

Returning to the station, we began to follow a broad tree-lined avenue. We walked fast, but a red double-decker bus quickly passed us by. Some children were playing with a ball and young couples were enjoying their time in the big grassy area of parkland on our right-hand side.

The scene was quite unexpected, because I remembered Soseki's words: 'The two years that I spent in London was the most unpleasant time of my life.'

His confession that he suffered from neurosis while living in London led me to believe that Clapham Common would be a gloomy place under a low grey sky, just as it was a hundred years ago.

I was relieved to find a bright scene where carefree people were having a good time.

I spoke again to two ladies walking together.

'Turn left at the red letter-box you see over there, and you will find yourself on that street.'

The red letter-box was built, I discovered later, in the Victorian period when Soseki lived. I wondered if Soseki had posted his letter to his wife in that same box.

After turning left at the letter-box as directed, a wide view of The Chase street came into view. At No. 81, I found a three-storeyed terraced house with a little garden. The same type of house lined both sides of the street.

I pushed the bell. I pushed it again and again, but there was no answer. There seemed to be no one in the house.

I had imagined Soseki would open the door and meet us, saying: 'You're welcome. You've travelled such a long distance.'

I may have cherished an illusion that I was now living life in the Meiji era.

We were at a loss, quite disappointed. Seeing our plight, a person who happened to pass by was kind enough to tell us that the museum was actually at the terraced house just across the street.

I felt so relieved and pushed the bell of the house numbered 80 B. We were ushered in and met Mr Ikuo Tsunematsu, the curator, who was there by himself. He was at his desk with a personal computer on it, overlooking No. 81. I had an impression that he always faced Soseki so that they could be united both mentally and physically.

While he was working in England, Mr Tsunematsu became an ardent admirer of Soseki. He eagerly told us that he had established the museum with his own money so that he might exhibit the vast amount of collected material concerning Soseki.

'I have been translating "*Inside the Glass Door*",' he observed.

I could not respond properly to his passion and erudition and made an inconsequential reply:

'I have had a great deal of difficulty in getting here. I nearly lost my way. . . .'

I had intended to convey my zeal, but my words were entirely off the point.

'You should have consulted the internet,' remarked Mr Tsunematsu, and the advice brought me back to reality. Why hadn't I thought of that?

The museum was a simple building, but the two rooms in it were piled high with books, and a substantial quantity of materials were on the walls. We would have stayed there longer if we had had enough time, but we had to leave after an hour.

Back in the street, I looked at No. 81. A blue plaque on the white wall stated: 'NATSUME SOSEKI 1867–1916 JAPANESE NOVELIST lived here 1901–1902'.

I took a picture of that, left the house and walked towards the Underground station, feeling as if my heart were left behind. We walked along the road by the park. This park must have been the place where Soseki practised riding a bicycle. I was lost in deep nostalgia.

I am not a Soseki specialist. Still, I wondered where this elevated feeling came from. I felt I had achieved something that other people had never attained. Like other tourists, I liked to see the sights of London – to enjoy an elegant tea at Fortnum & Mason, to go window-shopping at Harrods for famous brands. The little trip I went on to the Soseki Museum, fleeing from temptation, gave me such satisfaction as I had never experienced.

Mori Ogai, who studied in Germany seventeen years before Soseki, wrote about his romance with Eris in his '*Dancing Girl*'. Soseki did not lead such a gay life. Was his life in England as lonely as 'a shaggy dog in a group of wolves'? I wanted to look into his mind. That was what I thought as I walked feeling very tired.

Almost at the same time as our trip to England, I watched a television programme entitled 'To experience for yourselves in 1900 what Soseki experienced in a foggy town'.

He changed his boarding house five times including his last lodging in Clapham Common – sometimes to the south of the Thames and other times to the north. Each place still seems to retain some memory of Soseki. Moving five times in two years! I'd like to know the reason.

I got another fax from Ms K, saying:

'How I'd like to visit the other four boarding houses! When can we do that? Is it a mere dream?'

By all means, of course, I'd like to go again.

TRANSLATED BY N. KUMABE

47.

A Little Trip from Glasgow

Kayoko Nakamura

****

It is already three years since we visited Scotland, where my husband went on business. I knew very little about Scotland before the trip. It is entirely thanks to an old man named John that the country is so familiar to me.

Early in September it was chilly in the morning and evening, but it got so warm in the daytime that we could do without our coats. I went for a walk along one of Edinburgh's streets, wearing one shirt over another. The sound of bagpipes played for tourists is sometimes heard there. I feel both joy and sorrow at the sound and my blood begins to boil.

Just as Edinburgh is the centre of Scotland's politics, so Glasgow is that of its industry and commerce. On the evening of the third day of our trip, we took a train for Glasgow at Haymarket Station in Edinburgh. It was an hour's ride.

On the fourth day we headed for Kelvingrove Museum. On the way we saw some pupils playing in a primary school playground. They were in their uniforms of a dark blue sweater and a tartan skirt, quite characteristic of Scotland. We reached the museum in twenty minutes, but it was closed until March 2006 because it was under repair. We had to change our schedule at once. Such things often happen, which could not be known by the travel agency arranging the tour. I talked with my husband and we decided instead to visit a twelfth-century abbey in Paisley. We took an underground train from the nearby station to Central Station. Underground trains are surprisingly smaller than those in Tokyo.

Central Station was big. People gathered under the electronic notice-board to see which platforms they should go to. The notice-board said that the two trains bound for Paisley had been cancelled although the cause was not announced. Would our train really come? I was due to go to a concert given by the Royal Scotttish National Orchestra that evening and had arranged to meet my friend in the hall at seven o'clock. It was already a little before noon. I became anxious, when an old man carrying some large, heavy luggage on his shoulder spoke to me:

'Where are you going?'

'To Paisley,' I answered.

'I'm going to a station this side of Paisley. You'll be OK.'

That was perhaps what the old man said, as I remembered later. He spoke to me earnestly, looking into my eyes, but I could hardly make out what he was saying. I hear even Englishmen cannot understand some Scottish accents. I pretended I understood him and kept watching him, but the truth is, I could not understand. Then my husband whispered to me:

'I presume he means that he is doing Japanese *bonsai*.'

The old man knew that we were Japanese. I cannot tell how he knew it. Time passed moment by moment. We nearly decided not to go, when the old man took us to the station ticket office and asked them what had caused the delay to the trains. He looked stubborn. It might be characteristic of the Scotch disposition.

'The train is coming,' said a station attendant.

Pleased with this, the old man winked at me. I could no longer change my schedule. He spoke to me with heart and soul.

When the guard came round, the old man explained our situation and bought us our return ticket. How good-natured he was! He bagan talking of his family. He had six children and two grandchildren. He smiled a happy smile when he spoke of his grandchildren, who often said to him:

'Pocka money! Pocka money!'

I vaguely knew that he meant 'pocket money'. It was the first time that I understood his English and then we burst into laughter all together. He said he was very fond of Japan.

After about fifteen minutes he said:

'I'm getting off at the next station. I can see my house from the train.'

'My old friend, give me your address so that I may send you a Christmas card this year,' I said hurriedly.

He wrote with a trembling hand, 'Mr John Harris, Crookston, Glasgow, Scotland.'

'You are my first friend in Scotland,' I said, and he got off the train smiling.

The train left the tiny station of Crookston. I looked out of the window and unexpectedly found the old man raising his hands high and waving at the corner of a road. Standing up, my husband and I waved back. I realized I had failed to ask him what had made him like Japan.

In November after I returned to Japan, I suffered from a series of problems and, having lost my hearing in one ear, I had to go into hospital on my forty-ninth birthday. In December, I left hospital and was making efforts to restore my hearing, when I received a Christmas card from the old man together with a doll and a book introducing Scotland. How encouraged I was! I was with him for only a couple of hours, but he wrote to me addressing me as a dear friend in Japan. While recovering from my illness, I enjoyed reading the book about Scotland's history and listening to Scottish music.

Three years have now passed. The exchange of cards has continued between John and us. I sent him a picture of my daughter in kimono, who became an adult. John sent back a letter of congratulations. I wrote to him about Japanese kimono and told him that the kimono my daughter wore had been given me by my mother. Last year, he sent me a picture of the Highlands. I dream of visiting the place some day. A toast to John, a genuine Scotsman!

TRANSLATED BY N. KUMABE

48.

Sherlock Holmes Club

Yuki Tezuka

****

There are a great number of people who are studying Sherlock Holmes, the world-famous detective Conan Doyle created, believing that he really lived. They are called Sherlockians and there are a lot of Sherlock Holmes Societies all over the world. In this country, too, there is the Japan Sherlock Holmes Society which was founded in 1977.

Currently, the number of the members is about 1,000. There is no examination of the applicant's qualifications. The only indispensable requisite is that they love Sherlock Holmes. The members are expected to study a subject of their own choice regarding Sherlock Holmes and Britain.

Some members collect data, using a personal computer, and write about Holmes; others draw pictures or manga, making the best use of their talent. Still others talk with other Sherlockians over a cup of coffee or drinks, as Holmes supposedly did, and promote friendship, which also might be called a form of 'study'.

I for one have been carrying out research on Victorian London. When a book on Sherlock Holmes was written by members and published here in 1987, I contributed an essay on the currency system used in Victorian England, the sailing ships of those days and the buildings and sites remaining in London and associated with the stories, even though I was still a student inexperienced at writing essays.

The members are quite different from each other in interests and tastes. If I were not a member, I would not have got acquainted with Mr A, who is a railway fan, nor would I have talked with Mr B, who is studying chemistry. Their walks of life are so different from mine. However, the moment the key word 'Holmes' is put into the conversation, all the members begin to take part in it with shining eyes and talk about topics they are well versed in and listen to information that is new to them.

Those efforts accumulated over decades have borne fruit again. This year an 'Encyclopedia of Sherlock Holmes' has been published here. It consists of articles selected from published books and those newly written in response to the call. It has as many as 800 keywords.

Several years ago NHK (Japan Broadcasting Corporation) produced a special TV programme featuring Sherlock Holmes. I also took part in the show with other members, when someone said, 'It is a wonderful thing, isn't it, for such a great number of fully-fledged grown-ups to be so earnestly involved in making a study of one subject together.' The words exactly express what we are doing now.

The members include students, but generally speaking most of them are people of mature age. They are respectable members of society who pursue their callings in life. In the society there is no discrimination between members. A famous university professor is not privileged. An individual's title or status in a company means nothing.

From some critical point of view it may be a waste of time for such grown-ups to devote their energy to the detective stories, but we believe that pursuing our day-dreams all our life will give us a source of energy necessary for our everyday work and provide the spiritual nourishment essential for our life.

TRANSLATED BY S. KURAMOCHI

49.

Shakespeare's Minor Characters

Saburo Kuramochi

****

In this country, William Shakespeare has been popular for the past 150 years. The translation of his complete works was finished as early as 1928 and his plays have often been performed in Japanese. Now there are a great number of students of Shakespeare. I for one read some of his plays in English at university and have seen quite a few of his plays performed; I have also read English and Japanese books on the dramatist. Today, among the Japanese critics, I am personally most impressed with the view of Shakespeare by Rintaro Fukuhara (1894–1981).

Most people are fascinated by impressive characters like Hamlet, Othello and Macbeth, or Lady Macbeth, whereas Fukuhara shifts our attention towards minor characters who do not usually attract the audience's attention. He tells us that Shakespeare is a great dramatist in that he has created attractive marginal characters as well as commanding figures. A play cannot be complete without people who are not particularly important for the development of the plot.

One example is a messenger in *Romeo and Juliet.* An old man totters onto the stage in Act I. He is Capulet's servant. He is going to deliver the invitations to the feast to be given by his master, but he cannot read the address, because he is illiterate. He happens to come across Romeo and, saying to him, 'I pray, sir, can you read?' asks him to whom the invitations are addressed.

Romeo, sad at his unrewarded love towards Rosaline, answers that he can read 'mine own fortune in my misery' and then reads the address aloud and lets him know to whom the letters should be delivered. He incidentally finds his love's name among the guests, and decides to attend the feast, disguised by a mask. He sees Juliet there and falls in love with her.

The old man is such an inconsequential figure that he is not listed among the *dramatis personae*, but Fukuhara emphasizes that the scene is not only amusing but also pathetic and regrets that it is omitted in an English film based upon the play.

The illiterate man belongs to the class in which no one expects him to go to school and learn how to read and write. Actually he cannot read, but he is ordered by his master to deliver the invitations with the guest's name on them. He must ask others where to deliver. He is in an embarrassing situation.

No one wants to be illiterate. The messenger also wishes to read and write. He could read words if he had a chance to learn at school or elsewhere. Illiteracy is not history. Even today a number of countries are launching illiteracy eradication campaigns. The messenger scene in *Romeo and Juliet* makes us realize there are a lot of people in the world who neither read nor write.

Another example is an apothecary in Act V of the same play. Romeo goes to his shop to buy a dram of poison to kill himself after he hears that Juliet is dead. At first, the apothecary answers that it is prohibited to sell it on pain of death, but agrees to do so, saying, 'My poverty, not the will, consents.' He is too poor to observe Mantua's law. A hungry man cannot observe any law for that matter. As Romeo justly says to him, 'the world affords no law to make thee rich'. In the film, regrettably, the apothecary scene also is omitted. Romeo uses a dagger, instead of drinking poison, to kill himself. As a result, the audience cannot hear the poor man's pathetic words which contain an important message. It is not only the apothecary alone that is so poor and hungry as to violate the law.

A third example is Cinna at the end of Act III in *Julius Caesar* (which was translated into Japanese in 1884 in the midst of the democratic movement). The play impresses us with the fight for liberty, Brutus's noble character, Antony's skilful speech, while Fukuhara turns our attention to Cinna, the poet, a minor character not directly related with the main plot. The plebeians who are stirred to fury by Antony try to avenge the murder of Caesar and smoke out the conspirators. On the way to Caesar's funeral, Cinna is intercepted by them and is threatened with death, merely because his name is 'Cinna' by coincidence.

Cinna: Truly my name is Cinna.
Second Plebeian: Tear him to pieces; he's a conspirator.
Cinna: I am Cinna the poet, I am Cinna the poet.
Fourth Plebeian: Tear him for his bad verses, tear him for his bad verses.
Cinna: I am not Cinna the conspirator.
First Plebeian: It is no matter, his name is Cinna.

The truth is that there are the two Cinnas: Cinna the conspirator against Caesar and Cinna the poet. Cinna the poet is mistaken for Cinna the conspirator. In fact, there is no reason for murdering him at all, but plausible although baseless reasons are given. Cinna shall be killed for writing bad verse and for having the same name as one of the conspirators.

In a riotous situation, the rule of reason breaks down. When people are well past reason, anything can happen and anything can be justified. The life of an individual is at the mercy of the mob's caprice. Cinna will be fooled and torn to pieces as a fly is killed by a wanton boy. The scene seems to be comic, but really it is tragic.

There is a justifiable reason why great men such as Caesar or Brutus are murdered, but obscure persons are killed for no reason at all. It is not only Roman plebeians but also people in general who lose their reason and do unreasonable things when they are agitated and stirred up by dictators or propagandists.

Shakespeare's minor characters deserve attention, as Fukuhara insists. When we are ready to hear them, they tell us that there are still a lot of problems we must solve.

50.

We Japanese and the Past

Harumi Kimura

****

My acquaintance living in Kyoto, which is a city full of old temples, grumbles:

'The remarkable popularity of the song "In a Thousand Winds" has caused the Japanese temples to complain that burial plots in their graveyards do not sell well.'

What the popular song really means is that we should accept our death based on an animistic world view of human beings becoming unified with nature after death. But a large number of Japanese have misinterpreted the song believing it advocates scattering the bones of the dead instead of entombing them. I know a considerable number of people around me who do not want to be buried in the tomb with their own family. It is true that it costs a great deal to purchase and maintain a grave. Whereas, if the bones of a dead person are scattered, there is nothing more to be concerned about in the future. Scattering bones may sound rather romantic to those people, but its basic idea, in a way, is to throw away unnecessary things.

The deceased may remain unforgettable in the mind of one's family and friends, but shapeless things are to be forgotten as time goes by. We will keep remembering our deceased parents and brothers or sisters, but the existence of our ancestors is recognized only through tombstones or Buddhist memorial tablets. A most remarkable present trend is to throw away a link with past history and predecessors, and the popularity of that song may have prompted or even promoted the trend, although perhaps not intentionally. It seems to me that below the surface there is post-war individualism at play here.

A certain man – let us call him Mr A – had to deal with the death of his parents, and the parental house, which was a single-family house, with no one living in it. Other family members could not afford to buy the property, so they had to sell the house. But Mr A was distressed, because it was his ancestral home and the repository of so many childhood memories.

Mr A was quite affluent and purchased the house from his joint inheritors so that his newly-married son could live in it. He expected his son to be glad to live in the house of such distinctive character with its old associations and garden.

But the young couple had a different set of values. Weeding the garden, associating with neighbours and fastening the many wooden sliding doors of the house were seen as quite irksome tasks for them. In less than two months, they had moved to a flat, where one key was enough to secure their everyday life.

Mr A expected that the young generation's mind would be enriched by living in the ancestral home and becoming conscious of historical connections with the previous generations. What he intended to present to the couple was the value of continuity and keeping in touch with the past.

'Bringing up children has brought us no rewards,' a disappointed Mr A mutters despairingly.

That thought may lie at the root of the growing trend to have fewer or no children. Of course parents do not bring up children for what they get back. They are repaid enough by the pleasure of seeing their children grow up. But from the viewpoint of genealogy and its long time-span it is quite natural that parents should waver when they come to wonder what they are bringing up their children for. They might as well depend upon social welfare work in their old age, and reject the idea of making great efforts to leave a fortune to their descendants.

During my stay in England thirty years ago, I observed the English life-style which is ahead of today's Japan by thirty or forty years.

The English people's way of life is based on the unit of a married couple and it does not matter much whether or not they have children. While their children are young, they choose to live in towns where they can have easy access to schools and shops. The children usually leave home when they finish at secondary school, whether or not they go on to college, or university, or get a job. After the children leave home, the couple are free to get on with their own life; some may begin a rural life they have longed for. Once I visited a mansion which was a converted old water mill.

I enjoyed that fairy tale atmosphere such as might be seen in Constable's landscapes.

But such an elegant quality of life might not last long. As they grow old, the couple might have pains in many parts of their body. Their physical strength and faculties too could deteriorate so that they are unable to drive around. As a result, they would often have to leave the countryside, which is inconvenient to live in, even if it has scenic beauty. They would feel sad at leaving rural life, but they would choose to spend the last stage of their life in a town. This change of abode is, of course, their last move.

The English as a whole do not mind moving. A house does not belong to an individual, but is the common property of a society where people live in turn. The UK has a long history as a welfare state, where the aged are given homes according to their degree of weakness and need. To provide for their costs, they pay more than one-third of their income in tax.

There is a great difference between Japan and the UK. In Japan, houses are often destroyed when a generation changes, and are sold for tax payment and for dividing up. As a result there remains only a plot with no buildings on it. In such cases we can hardly remember what building stood there yesterday. In Britain, on the other hand, houses, once built, generally stand as they are for hundreds of years. We can even visit a house where Shakespeare used to live. If it is haunted by a ghost, it has even more value. When the British move to a very old house, they give less priority to the value of living comfortably, more to experiencing the past which the house still retains within its walls, even if they may experience some inconvenience in living there.

The English live deeply soaked in the past which they share as a nation, though only the nobility can trace back their own ancestors who really existed in that past. The common people live in an old house in an old town, bathed in the past as if in ozone. Their mind is reassured and enriched by accepting the so-called human fatality.

The trend towards the nuclear family may be seen both in Japan and the UK, but the Japanese sense of the past in their life is so different from that of the English. The difference concerns the depth of thought in their daily life. Japan is on its way to becoming a welfare state like the UK, but how to take in the sense of the past into daily life seems to be a problem as far as one's state of mind is concerned.

The readers of this book will recognize, however, that, though houses in Japan are continually being rebuilt, leaving nothing of the past, we Japanese are surrounded by many different aspects of an ancient invisible heritage in our everyday lives. Some people, for example, are interested in Zen, some in tea ceremony, some enjoy going to kabuki. The older we grow, the more we would like to make contact with traditions in one way or another. The point is that we have to make a conscious effort to do that, living as we do in very new, modern houses.

PART 7

FROM THE KITCHEN WINDOW

51.

Ten Years in this Town

Yukiko Nishida

****

We started living in the town of Koenji in Tokyo ten years ago when I was in my early fifties.

We were looking around for a house where we could live with my husband's 88-year-old mother who was then living alone in Kanazawa in central Japan. When we saw our present house on the recommendation of a young real estate agent, my husband and I agreed at once that this was the place for us. We were quite taken with the camellia and maple trees that were growing in the very small garden.

The house has access to two railway lines, a Japan Railways (JR) line and an underground line. It is also near the local shopping street, connecting the JR station and the underground station. The street, about a fifteen-minute-walk from one end to the other, is lined on both sides with shops.

Two rather chic boutiques with wide storefronts stood side by side about halfway along the street. A red hibiscus pot was placed in front of the glass door of one of the boutiques. All the other shops in the street had narrow fronts of less than two metres or three-and-a-half metres at most, so when you arrived in front of these two shops, you felt as though the street had become wider and brighter. Both boutiques displayed clothes with extremely expensive price tags in their shop windows; the prices were such that I felt there was almost one digit too many. Although I didn't buy anything, I always enjoyed looking at the clothes, which gave me a feeling of luxury.

We lived with my mother-in-law for less than three years. We left her in my brother-in-law's care when my husband was transferred to Maebashi in the north-west of Tokyo, where we spent the next two-and-a-half years. Now that we have come back to Tokyo and started living in Koenji again, we feel the rapid changes taking place in the shopping street almost on a daily basis. One of the two boutiques closed down earlier this year and a very ordinary general store appeared in its place, leaving only the boutique with the hibiscus pot.

Before I knew it, general stores and second-hand clothes shops mushroomed in the shopping street, and young people descended on the town and headed for these shops in droves every weekend. The street today is full of young couples holding hands, as well as groups of young men and women chatting and joking with each other.

The biggest bookshop in the street closed down a year ago. I used to go there regularly to buy magazines and paperbacks, so I was quite upset. The shop always seemed to be full of customers, but were they all just browsing? The bookshop has turned into a chemist's selling other goods also, one of those nationwide chain stores. Whenever I pass by, it is brightly lit with miscellaneous everyday goods piled up high along the shop front. I suppose it is, in a way, a scene of abundance. In no time, I was buying cat food or a nutrition supplement or two in passing, finding it convenient.

The sushi restaurant we patronized closed down, too. I used to like their Osaka sushi, the small rectangular sushi pressed into shape in wooden boxes. The restaurant had just been renovated, but for some reason the spruced-up interior attracted fewer customers than before. The sushi restaurant has now become a discount opticians. Who knows? I may be buying new glasses there someday.

Soon after that, one of the flower shops in the street closed down. This surprised me because it was managed by two middle-aged couples and appeared to be doing the most business of the several flower shops in the street.

Two days after the flower shop closed down, a perfumery opened in its place. A changeover this rapid is rare. Though it specializes in perfume, its main draw is perfume priced at about 500 yen a bottle, targeting young people. Can it continue to attract customers or is it soon going to be renovated to become yet another new shop? No one knows what lies ahead.

Koenji, a town crowded with hundreds of shops, of course has many shops which have not changed in the last ten years. The grocery shop at the corner of the traffic lights is one of them. When I see the middle-aged couple energetically laying out fresh vegetables, I feel relieved. At the chemist's next door, I often see the middle-aged pharmacist chatting with her customers. I myself go to her for minor injuries or a cold.

The kimono shops, both large and small, are still thriving. Some shops are constantly changing their display of high quality kimonos, but some shops are old and small. When I once bought a pair of *tabi*, or Japanese-style socks, and a *han-eri*, a detachable collar for the kimono, at the small, old shop, the shopkeeper said, 'I'm eighty and I can't see very well.' She shuffled about the shop and sold me the goods.

Perhaps these shops will be able to stay in business thanks to the Koenji Awa-odori, or Awa Dance Festival, held in our town every summer. I am sure they are supplying the costumes worn by the participants.

The Awa Dance Festival, held on the last weekend in August, is a two-day event that draws more than a million visitors. Our son who lives in another part of Tokyo brought a friend to see the event this year. To watch the dancing parade, they stationed themselves on the other wider street stretching straight from the JR station. They later told us that though it was crowded, the dancers appeared relaxed as they spread out along the wide street. They were impressed.

Avoiding the crowds, my husband and I went to our narrow shopping street and stood in front of the general store to watch the parade. The *ohayashi* drummers playing Japanese carnival music passed by, beating their drums at full blast. They were followed by children wearing make-up, skilfully waving their hands in the *otoko odori*, or men's dance. Then came the women, donning *sugegasa*, or sedge hats, and pink *kedashi*, or underskirts, and dancing along elegantly with their hands held up high.

My thoughts flitted back to the day we watched the dance with our mother-in-law, who was then in a wheelchair. It is already four years since she passed away.

Here I am, I thought, still living in this town that continues to thrive, flexibly changing its face little by little to suit the times.

TRANSLATED BY H. MIYAZAKI AND Y. TAKAHASHI

52.

Weeding as an Icebreaker

Michiyo Sasaki

****

It was a heat-wave alright. The maximum temperature topped 30 degrees Celsius for a few days, then 35 degrees for another few days. The mercury continued to skyrocket after that; 39 degrees was recorded in a town in Saitama, just north of Tokyo, the day before yesterday, and it finally hit 40 degrees yesterday.

I had some errands to do in Omiya and went out during the day. It is less than a ten-minute walk to the station, but the heat rising from the concrete got to me and I felt my thinking power declining rapidly. After only twenty minutes or so of running errands, I was so thirsty and exhausted that I couldn't take it any more. I had to rush into a fast food outlet where I gulped down a large cup of iced tea.

I cancelled another errand I had in nearby Urawa and beat a hasty retreat back home. I was planning to go out that night, so I needed to rest a little and recuperate from the heat.

That night, I had dinner with friends whom I hadn't met for a long time, and we caught up on each other's news and talked about our past times. Thoroughly relaxed, I headed home a little after nine. Though the evening air was still hot, the temperature had dropped considerably. I was waiting for the lights to change at the intersection of Route 17 near our house when a neighbour who lives on the same floor of the condominium came and stood beside me. He then spoke to me.

'Hello, there'.

'Oh, hello. Isn't it hot? It went up to 40 degrees today.'

'Yes, this scorching heat has been going on for a while but we were lucky, weren't we, that the weeding day was a cool day?'

The man spoke softly, with an air of an intellectual gentleman.

A weeding day was organized in our community five days ago in preparation for the summer festival. If we let things slide, the park and flowerbeds around our condominium and the square beside the athletics ground become full of weeds in no time, so we are called together for a weeding session several times a year.

The residents of our condo were called up, too, but most of us didn't know each other at all. So one of the residents in charge of the weeding that day suggested that the residents of the condo work together as much as possible, partly to get to know each other better.

While we were weeding and also during break time, we talked about the upcoming repair work of the condo and the finances of managing the condo, but we also enjoyed chatting about harmless topics such as travelling and drinking. I hit it off with one woman in particular as we talked about our families and our children. She even promised to take me one of these days to the municipal swimming pool she goes to. I had talked to the man now standing next to me, just a nodding acquaintance till then, for the first time at the weeding.

After crossing the street, I felt a little uncomfortable walking side by side with a person I didn't know well, so I said, 'Please go ahead if you are in a hurry', but he replied, 'No, I'm not in any hurry.' We were walking at the same pace. It was a five-to-six-minute walk back to the condo and I felt it was unnatural and uncomfortable to keep silent all the way. I recalled that during the weeding he had laughingly said, 'I never go without a drink, all 365 days of the year. I can't live without alcohol.'

'Isn't beer delicious when it's hot like this? Weren't you saying the other day that you can't let a day pass by without a drink?'

'I limit myself to one glass of beer at lunchtime as I have to go back to work. But after work, I drink with my friends. I emptied three bottles today.'

He didn't look drunk and in the night-time lighting I couldn't tell if his face was a little red or not.

'I don't drink much but when the temperature goes over 30 degrees, I feel like drinking beer because it tastes so delicious. The first glass is especially good.'

'Oh, really? I have to drink a glass of beer first to work up an appetite. When it's hot like this, nothing beats beer.'

'When the temperature is around 25 degrees, I don't crave beer that much. I think beer tastes better when you drink it outside, in a beer garden, than in an air-conditioned room.'

I went on, all the while thinking I might be talking a little too much. But he continued talking in a friendly way.

'You may be right. Come to think of it, we chill our beer until it's ice cold here in Japan, but in Germany they don't chill it so much and in Britain they don't chill beer at all.'

'I didn't notice that in Britain but I remember it was like that in Germany. Maybe that's why the beer tasted so good even when the temperature was not over 30 degrees. It was because the beer was not chilled so much.'

'Yes, that could be the reason.'

His cheerful conversation might be attributed to the several drinks he had had, but I was unusually chatty myself although I don't know whether it was the effect of the 40 degrees heat I was hit with during the day or the lingering euphoria of the dinner with my friends.

I recalled my childhood when neighbours used to enjoy the evening breeze together. In those days, neighbourly ties were much stronger than they are today. It must be my age which enabled me to talk casually about beer-drinking with a man I didn't know so well. His wife, who never smiles at anyone, is always smiling when she is with him, so he must be a good husband.

Thanks to the weeding day, I now have one more neighbour I can talk with.

TRANSLATED BY H. MIYAZAKI AND Y. TAKAHASHI

53.

Lifelong Learning in my Town

Keiko Otake

****

'Good Morning.'

After greeting other people in the classroom, I sat down in my seat. Here in this room, every Sunday we have lectures at around 10.30 in the morning for about two hours. The lectures are run by the Kichijoji Sonritsu Zatsugaku Daigaku. This unique name means, 'A learning place created by people who reside in the community of Kichijoji'.

The town of Kichijoji, where I live, was developed by the people who escaped from the Meireki fire that occurred in central Tokyo during the Edo period. Today, Kichijoji is a large shopping district. The school was established for the purpose of appreciating and recognizing the origin of the town and also to create a meeting place that would foster friendship.

The administration of the school is not overseen by the local government, but by the citizens of Kichijoji. Because of this, there is no charge for anything. The travel agency is letting us use a room on the second floor of their building and lecturers volunteer to speak there.

The lecturers vary from an elderly woman teaching how to make her 'special' homemade pickles to a world famous spider expert talking about his specialty. These lecture programme has been running for twenty-nine years, and today is the 1401st lecture. To listen to the lectures, you do not need to go through any procedures or submit any paperwork. You just have to write your name in the attendance register.

The first time I attended a lecture was three years after the school started. The lecture was entitled, 'How to Brew Good Coffee', and was given by the owner of the Café Mocha that is in the town. At the end of the lecture, the café owner provided free coffee for the forty-odd listeners. The café was famous for making rich coffee. I remember I went to the lecture with my own coffee cup in hand.

One day I talked about 'The History and Uses of Tea'. I chose this theme because I have enjoyed the tea ceremony for a long time. To prepare for the lecture, I went out to a second-hand bookshop in Kanda. I looked for an old book and collected materials. Together with my university student daughter, we provided powdered green tea while wearing kimonos and were well received. We gave the audience the sweets for the day which were dried persimmons that had been sent by my mother who lives in my hometown. I also added some sweet chestnuts that I had made.

Since then, I often listen to the lectures and, once or twice a year, I also give lectures on topics that interest me. I only do this after thorough research. I usually don't try to understand things I am not interested in, but if I attend these lectures, I absorb information even without meaning to. Because my curiosity is stronger than other people's, I have been going regularly to the lectures.

My husband, who is seventy-three years old and going to work only three days a week now, has started attending the lectures as a result of my recommendation. When I can't attend, he goes alone. When he comes home, he tells me about the day's lecture with great animation and feeling. His friends from the lectures have become his irreplaceable 'best' friends without his noticing.

The people attending the lectures are mostly men. There are usually about fifteen people in the audience and sometimes there is someone who falls asleep, but that is allowed. After the lecture is finished, there is time to ask questions. Each story, such as T-san's about her unimpeded trips to sixty-three countries, or the ninety-year-old man's about his business trip to Australia to purchase sand, has its unique personality. There is always cultural exchange between lecturers and the audience and that is also very interesting.

Today we have a special university class. One of our students, Tatsuzo Murakami, is going to be given a 'Degree in random knowledge'. He will also give a lecture to commemorate the event. He comes out in his cap and satin costume. They give him his degree and flowers and he starts to speak. The theme of the lecture is: 'Dwelling on letters and words for several decades'. There are many difficult *kanji* written on the board, and English and German words are there as well. He explains the origin of the letters and the words. I raise my hat to him for the freshness of the knowledge he conveys. Today he celebrates his ninetieth birthday.

This is a 'Handmade University for the community to enjoy'. I think this is the ideal for lifelong learning.

TRANSLATED BY P. HALTMAN

54.

From the Kitchen Window

Sachiko Mibu

****

I live on the first floor of a three-storied condominium building that houses six families. My parents' house was rebuilt in this way some twenty years ago. On each floor, there is a relatively big apartment for families and a small single's apartment for rent.

My mother-in-law moved into the small apartment on our floor about ten years ago. She had been living alone for a long time but had been unwell for a while and may have been feeling a little weak. When we suggested that she move into the small apartment which had become vacant at the time, she accepted our offer eagerly and moved in without delay.

The condominium building is L-shaped and faces a small garden. From our kitchen window, I could see the living-room and bedroom of my mother-in-law's apartment. Every morning and every evening, it became my daily routine to look out of the window while doing the dishes at the sink and check whether her curtains were open or closed. Even if we didn't see each other every day, I could tell whether she was up and about or not. I found this highly convenient.

When my husband and I got married thirty years ago, we started our life as newly-weds in an apartment next to our parents-in-law. That condominium building was a much larger building housing many families. Our apartment on the ground floor faced a garden, like this one. My father-in-law, who had already retired, would sometimes appear all of a sudden from the garden and, taken unawares, I would jump up from the sofa where I was lying down having a nap. He must have been happy to have a young bride around and eager to take care of us. I can understand that now but at the time, I was young and I used to complain about this to my husband.

Checking on my mother-in-law from the kitchen window, I would recall those bygone days.

When my mother-in-law moved into the one-bedroom apartment, after having disposed of most of her enormous amount of belongings, she was in very poor health but she got better day by day. She came and dined with us every weekend and it was a great pleasure for me to hear her say that she had never been healthier in all her life. Seven years passed in this way, during that time, although she was hospitalized and operated on twice for fractures of the femur.

But the year before last, in the spring, a tumour was found in her colon and the doctor's diagnosis was that an operation was no longer possible. We did not tell her what the diagnosis was. She got through the summer, but by the end of the summer when evening cicadas began to sing, the curtains of her room remained drawn more often than before. She no longer had the strength to walk to the window and open the curtains.

In mid-September, she was admitted to hospital. The following morning, I looked out of the kitchen window towards my mother-in-law's apartment, as I always did, and saw the window that she would never open again. When all the leaves of our garden had shed their leaves, my mother-in-law passed away.

I was clearing up the apartment, renovating it and was about to start looking for a tenant when our son informed us of his marriage plans. Unexpectedly, the young couple decided to move into the apartment vacated by my mother-in-law. Listening to the requests from our son for a dishwasher or more electric points, I recalled the last years of my mother-in-law's life. I reflected on the fact that she had never made any requests of any kind, and, with bitter regret, I wished I had been more concerned about ensuring she was comfortable.

The young couple started their new life. They were both working and seemed to be busy and the curtains often remained drawn in the morning. One day, I noticed that the usually closed window was open and that the television was on. I learned later that my daughter-in-law was not feeling well and had not gone to work that day. This went on for a few days and the curtains were open every day. She didn't seem to get better. Almost a month later, we were told that she was pregnant.

From that day, I began to look out of the window every morning again. Were the curtains open or drawn? It had never occurred to me that I would be worried about that window again, but I couldn't help being anxious about my daughter-in-law. I made some vichyssoise for her as she couldn't eat at all. I remembered that this was the only thing my mother-in-law could eat when she was in hospital and had lost all her appetite.

While I was making the soup, the memory of the day we buried my mother-in-law came back to me. Looking down at the family grave with the children, it had occurred to me then that the next time the grave is opened, it will be for my husband or for me. I had felt suddenly very old. The children will bury us as we buried my mother-in-law. I felt depressed that day as the day of my burial seemed to loom near.

But there I was, making some soup, still worrying about the children and taking care of them. I decided that my burial day was still far off. One day in the future, the children may start getting anxious about whether our curtains are drawn or not. Then so be it. I may raise the white flag and ask for help.

For some reason, this thought cheered me up as I poured the soup into cups in the kitchen.

TRANSLATED BY H. MIYAZAKI AND Y. TAKAHASHI

55.

Blue Daisies as a Mother's Day Present

Saki Ushido

****

On Mother's Day, my daughter and son–from their primary school days until they were grown up–have usually given me a modest present such as a carnation and a cake. Although they are not expensive presents, I am satisfied with them, because it is by no means certain that I would be satisfied with the presents when I get them. To buy expensive presents would be a waste of money, especially if I were not pleased with them.

On Mother's Day this year, I was a little happier than on previous occasions, because I was asked what flower I wanted as the present. The truth is, however, what I most want now is not a present. To be frank, I do not like their easygoing way of thinking that they can repay their debt of gratitude simply through the formality of giving a present.

It is a long time since I started doing housework, and even now I am not particularly good at it. I wish from the bottom of my heart I could be free from such work for an entire day just once in a blue moon, especially because I do not believe housework is my vocation.

For many years it has been my longstanding dream to wake up and find that breakfast is ready on the table and that someone has taken my place as a housewife for the whole day. Someone will say that I ought to have a break and go on a trip; but I am afraid I would not feel relaxed, since during that time I would be driven by my usual schedule from morning till night.

Several years ago, I lived alone in the house for a week, because my husband went off on a business trip and my children went away on an excursion. I prepared the meals, did the laundry and went shopping just for myself. In fact, I did almost the same things as usual during the week, but I enjoyed a relaxing time. I practised Japanese penmanship. I made a chart of my TV viewing schedule, including the programme names and the broadcast times and followed the schedule without interference from anyone. Enveloped in an atmosphere of freedom, I enjoyed an uplifting feeling of happiness.

That was because, for the first time since my marriage, I was entirely relieved of a housekeeper's, wife's and mother's obligations after I had been working for so many years without taking a rest. Sometimes I told my daughter about my feelings and views as a housewife so often that she seemed to understand me, but she was not willing to take my place and do the housework.

When the children were too busy to remember Mother's Day, my husband, reading my mind, kindly said to me, 'Shall we dine out? Today is Mother's Day'. But, though feeling grateful to him, I was unwilling to do so, thinking to myself 'Don't try and take the children's place, please. I am not your mother.'

On Mother's Day this year, we, my husband, my daughter and I went to a garden plant fair held near my house. Saplings of dogwoods, maple trees and gold crests were displayed for sale. Near them there were a lot of pots of pink dwarf carnations. My husband seemed to be urging my daughter to buy a pot of dwarf carnations as a Mother's Day present. My daughter had already bought a cake, however, so she looked slightly sullen and was unwilling to buy it. Nevertheless, she asked me which flower I liked.

Seizing the opportunity, I said, 'Thank you very much. I would love to have those blue daisies.'

I had been attracted by some varieties of blue daisies, which were on display beside the pots of dwarf carnations.

'Quite all right, as long as they please, Mum.'

In this way, to my great joy, I got a pot of pretty daisies with conspicuously blue flowers.

My daughter looked happy because I was pleased with her present. My husband looked dissatisfied only because I did not choose a carnation, as I have always done. He did not interfere, though, since the interested parties were satisfied, and walked a few steps apart from us.

I was happy that day, because my cherished desire, although I did not clearly express it, was accepted by my daughter. The best thing for me was to get what I wanted, even though it was not a traditional present.

Not wanting to take part in family celebrations recently, my son does not give me anything. But he helps me by willingly giving advice concerning personal computers and other electric appliances which he understands very well. My daughter helps me with housework, although she does not yet take my place.

What I hope for now is that they will help me in everyday life, instead of simply observing Mother's Day by going through the formality of giving presents.

TRANSLATED BY S. KURAMOCHI

56.

In Twenty-five Years

Yasuko Matsumoto

****

These days, it is no longer rare for women to work on an equal footing with men even in Japan. In my husband's company, too, women go on business trips abroad or are given overseas assignments. In fact, people are sent anywhere in the world regardless of gender. The company even has an in-house nursery.

I know this is the trend in society at large, but I am still astonished at this change. I used to work for this company myself twenty-five years ago, so the change surprises me even more.

I joined the company in 1981, five years before the introduction of the Equal Employment Act. It was a general trading company that dealt with a wide variety of goods 'from ramen noodles to aeroplanes'. It was a company with a history of over a hundred years which also prided itself on its relaxed and open atmosphere. With its high-powered businessmen flying all over the world, the company had the image of being at the forefront of the times. I don't think any other company in those days had a policy of sending women overseas for a period of three years.

Nevertheless, women were assigned to do 'clerical work' and worked as assistants to the men who were assigned to do 'comprehensive work'. Both the pay scale and the promotion system were totally different for men and women. All this was explained to us clearly at the company information meeting before we joined.

I went to co-educational schools from kindergarten to university, in a world where there was no discrimination between men and women and where girls got better grades than boys more often than not. So this was my first encounter with the real world.

Some of my friends were turned off by these old-fashioned ideas and looked for other jobs. Even then, women could work on an equal footing with men in some places, such as foreign companies and new companies, although they were small in number. But taking on the same job as men meant doing everything from cold-call sales without any appointment to working overtime until late at night. I was not prepared for that and nor was I fluent enough in English to be able to work in a foreign company. In the end, I chose this company where the salary was better than the other companies and the benefit package was good.

My first task every morning was to wipe the desks clean and make tea for everyone.

'Do this calculation, please.'

'I want you to send this telex to New York.'

I dealt with any work that my boss assigned me. Sometimes someone else would stop me and ask, 'Miss, will you make a copy of this?' Even when this irritated me, I smiled as I took the paper.

The manager who had just come back from the US was different from the others. He was of the opinion that women should utilize their abilities, too, and he once gave me a job that he would normally assign to a man. This was something that I had been waiting for, but the frustration that I felt somewhere deep inside did not disappear. However hard I worked on this job, I belonged to the category of women assigned to 'clerical work' and my status was not going to change. The personnel and pay systems were different for men and women. I could not resolve this dilemma.

The company's overseas operations were something that I was secretly aiming for ever since I decided to join the company. The location of these overseas operations were cities where women could safely live alone such as London, Düsseldorf and Hong Kong. It was a three-year assignment to which we were eligible to apply and take the test after we had been with the company for three years. On returning to Japan, I would be twenty-eight years old. In those days, twenty-five was considered to be the appropriate age for a woman to marry. Christmas cakes can be sold on 24 and 25 December but after the 25th, they can't be sold even at half price.

'Well, girls are the same. You have to do something about it by the time you're twenty-five or you'll be in big trouble. I'm joking, of course.' I heard this story from several men in the office and you could tell from their eyes that they weren't joking at all. The Christmas cake story quickly deflated my dreams of working overseas.

The men often talked about another marriage-related topic. 'It's not actually a rule,' they would start as a preamble and then go on to say, 'But when you marry someone in the company, one of you must leave.' This 'one of you' is of course the woman. In this company, employees were often transferred to different locations, and the company wanted the family to relocate with the employee. A working spouse would not be able to accompany the employee, and that is why two cannot work for the same company. That was how the system was explained to us, but the reasoning sounded a little forced. The real reason was probably something like: 'If women work for four or five years when they are young and single, that is more than enough.'

It so happened that I actually ended up leaving the company after four years because I met my husband who was working in the same department and we decided to get married. I didn't protest crying out, 'Why does one of us have to leave?' I left without making any fuss. Women are for 'clerical work', leftover 'Christmas Cakes' and the 'unwritten rule about marriage within the company'. Perhaps I had been gradually brainwashed ever since joining the company.

The unwritten rule about marriage seemed to have existed until the company officially announced its abolition fifteen years later.

Some women of my generation who have lived through the same times have continued working and are active in society today. If I had held onto my dream, a different route may have opened up for me, too, but I gave up my dream of my own accord. I let myself be influenced by the world around me and just drifted along.

But it is also true that Japanese society was like that at the time. I was aware of many situations around me that would now be considered sexual harassment and subject to litigation.

A great change has taken place in the last twenty-five years. I would like to give my heartfelt support to the women of today who are working on an equal footing with men. I will try to contain my feelings of envy.

TRANSLATED BY H. MIYAZAKI AND Y. TAKAHASHI

57.

Looking at My Mother from Behind

Yasuko Matsumoto

****

When my mother became ill, I often accompanied her on her hospital visits. The waiting-room was full of elderly people. Seeing an old lady unsteady on her feet supporting her equally ageing husband, I could not help feeling sorry for their plight.

'I'm so glad you are here,' my mother would say to me repeatedly. She has three daughters but my older sister, who lives with my mother, is a full-time junior high school teacher with a very busy schedule every day, and my younger sister lives in the United States. My husband is overseas on an assignment, without the family. I chose to stay in Japan for our children's education. Otherwise, I would have been out of the country, too. It was probably because she had this in mind that my mother kept saying, 'I'm so glad you are here.'

The doctor's diagnosis was that the aorta leading to my mother's heart had become swollen and could burst at any moment. The condition called for surgery to replace the damaged part of the aorta with a synthetic blood vessel. My mother was still well in control of her faculties and could have made it to her hospital appointments without anyone accompanying her. Even so, with my father gone, I felt that a serious illness such as this was just too big a burden for my 78-year-old mother to carry all by herself. I was glad that I could be there for her, too.

My mother would always add in a low voice: 'It's much better to have a young daughter accompanying you than an old woman like me seeing the doctor alone. The doctor's attitude is different.' Was this really so? It was hard to believe that doctors changed their way of examining patients according to the person accompanying the patient. On top of that, this daughter of hers could not really be called young. But my mother did not listen to my protests, firmly convinced that she was right.

My mother seems to have lost confidence in herself lately. Now and again, she would murmur sadly, 'I've become such an old woman. . . .'

Indeed, her hair has turned increasingly white and she seems to have become one size smaller. She may not have achieved anything that would be handed down to posterity, but she has led a life she need not be ashamed of, always putting her family first, ahead of herself. She still has great curiosity about everything and she is very studious. Her account of her life when she was a young woman during and after the war is full of episodes that would make a good book, if someone took the time to write them down. Is it so painful to experience the decline in one's appearance and physical strength? I try to speculate what must be going on in my mother's mind, but I realize that it is probably something you can't really understand until you reach that age yourself.

My mother underwent surgery, that lasted seven-hours, and after spending six days in the Intensive Care Unit, she returned to her hospital room. We were all happy to see her back, but the ten days or so after she was released from the ICU were most difficult for her. She could not move as she wanted to and could not do anything by herself. She had no appetite. She was still a little muddled at times, not fully conscious yet. She was exhausted in both mind and body. I thought she would feel freer to make more demands on me than on anyone else, so I went to visit her in the hospital as much as possible, setting aside all my other duties for the time being.

I recalled the time my mother was attending to my grandmother when she was hospitalized, more than twenty years ago. My grandmother had already begun to show signs of dementia then. She would call my mother, her own daughter, 'big sister', pull out the tube for the intravenous drip, or insist on going home. My mother felt she could not leave my grandmother alone in that condition, so she spent many nights in the hospital room, singing children's songs with my grandmother time and time again. Those songs were about the only things my grandmother seemed to remember well.

At the time, I was young, enjoying my youth, and totally absorbed in what I was doing. On a rare Sunday, I would be asked to take my grandmother's laundry back to the hospital, but busy with my own activities, I begrudged that chore. I remember, with bitter regret, how my father scolded me severely for not caring more about the family.

Now, years later, I am a parent myself, and I, too, have learned to control my own desires and put my family before myself. I feel I can spend time with my mother, unhurried and at ease. I have finally reached this stage myself. But I am still not quite prepared. I have not yet attained the maturity my mother displayed when she was attending to my grandmother.

The first days after my mother came back to her hospital room, I often witnessed scenes that startled me and made me wonder whether it was the onset of dementia.

'This room is full of insects.' My mother would raise her arms feebly and try hard to catch the insects. No insects were in sight anywhere. My mother's vacant expression overlapped with the expression of my grandmother, but I later learned that seeing many insects flying about was a symptom called 'eye-floater'. Then, there was the time when my mother began to say that she could see colourful spiral-looking things when she closed her eyes. The doctor explained to us that this was delirium, a sort of illusion caused by the anaesthetic used in the surgery.

My fears of dementia were proved wrong this time, but my fears may come true one day. . . . Would I be able to deal with my mother gently and patiently as my mother had done with her own mother, my grandmother? I am sorry to say that I am not yet ready. Here I am, still afraid of such a thought.

My mother is walking ahead of me. Looking at her from behind, tracing her steps and thoughts one by one, I gradually grow older myself.

TRANSLATED BY H. MIYAZAKI AND Y. TAKAHASHI

58.

First Love

Takako Yasugi

****

My bar, known as Ashibi, near Tsurumi Station, opens at 7.00 pm. Most of the customers usually go to eat and drink at a different restaurant or bar first and so they come to me afterwards. One night, however, when the cherry blossoms started to fall and it was chilly, the first arrival was unusually early. This is a very rare event in my bar. It happened to be the president of company K.

'Oh, you are most welcome! Are you alone? That's very unusual.' Without answering my question, he sat down with a rigid face. He started, 'I came here to let you know, because I feel this is my duty. . . .' The moment he started, I had a bad premonition, thinking that maybe it was about my schoolmate S, who had worked at Company K. After taking a sip of his whisky on the rocks, the president continued. 'From the beginning, Mr S did not like doctors. At the beginning of January last year, he couldn't bear his stomach pain any longer and he went to the hospital. As a result, he found out that he had stomach cancer and that an operation was not possible. Supposedly, he is numbing the pain with morphine.'

According to the president, he went to the hospital to see him, but S's slim body had become even thinner. He also said that S held his hand with a boney one. Concerned about the company, S asked how it was doing and if all was going well. His voice was very weak, but the power of his grip showed his strong interest and his feeling of guilt for not being able to assist with it. He asked the president to ask his wife about his condition. That was what the president told me in one breath.

After I heard this story from the president, S left the world forever. I am grateful to the president for telling me about it, because I was able to go to the wake to say goodbye to S. The dead man in the photograph looked very fashionable with his trademark Ascot tie. When I put my hands together to pray for him, I felt as if he understood my unspoken feelings towards him.

S and I were in the same high school. We had never spoken because we were never in the same class. The only thing I could do was to watch him from afar. He was very fashionable compared to the other boys. His white turtleneck sweater and dark blue trench coat with the tight belt were particularly nice. Looking back now, his face was like one of those illustrations by Junichi Nakahara (a famous illustrator at the time). My heart leapt up whenever I was in the same train carriage or bus while going to or coming home from school. I couldn't sleep late in the morning and always woke up excited. In the afternoon, my friends told me I was like a fire engine. As soon as class ended, I ran out the door.

I knew from one of my friends that S had joined Company K's, main division at their Tokyo headquarters. But time passed without my thinking about him. When we reached our sixtieth year, I met him at our high school class reunion party and was surprised that he had been transferred to the Tsurumi branch office which was very close to my bar. He seemed to be ageing well and looked very calm.

Once I talked about S to people from Company K when they came to my bar saying, 'I can tell you this because it happened a long time ago and I am drunk right now.' Since that day, the story about him came up very often. People always said something like, 'He is very good at golf and such a gentleman.' Even after his death, everyone talks about him like that. They say that I couldn't have helped falling in love with him. This is always the topic when people come to my bar to drink.

When S retired, he came to the bar with his colleagues and it was such an unexpected event, I forgot how time had passed. We sang the karaoke duet, 'I won't let you go tonight', and we danced. He said to me, 'It was a great night thanks to my boss who introduced me to Ashibi.' He also said, 'I will come again.' That was one year before he died.

TRANSLATED BY P. HALTMAN

59.

Tidying up

Yasuko Matsumoto

****

My 76-year-old mother and my 78-year-old mother-in-law are both busy sorting out their belongings these days. They say they want to tidy up their personal belongings while they can, before they grow senile.

My mother sighs saying that although she is busily working at it, she can't seem to get to the end of it and she finds herself exhausted every day. Half jokingly but half seriously, I say: 'You can leave things as they are. After you die, I'll do it for you and throw away everything that's left.'

I want her to enjoy herself doing the things she can while she is well rather than spend her time sorting things out. But my mother does not feel that way and she protests in earnest: 'If I leave it to you, you will throw away all the good things, too. I'm trying so hard to sort things out now because I don't want that to happen.'

My mother seems to have a lot of those good things and I think I'll be at a loss if she were to leave all those things behind, saying they are not to be thrown away. But feeling that it is not the time for such an uncalled-for comment, I just look on.

My husband's mother, who lives in Kyushu, is more thorough in her tidying-up. She has been an orderly person in all ways. For fifty years of her married life she kept her household accounts in a large thick notebook, and she has many notebooks filled with her neat figures on every page. If we say we will be leaving at ten o'clock, she will be ready by nine-forty.

So naturally my mother-in-law's house is always in perfect order. At least to me it looks perfect. I wonder what else she can do about the house, but it seems she still has many things to tidy up.

A few months ago, my mother-in-law sorted out her photos. Of course the photos were all already in albums. But the albums themselves had become old and some had even changed colour, so she bought new albums and put only the photos she wanted to keep in the new albums. That meant she threw away nearly half the photos.

My mother-in-law seems to have been engaged in this task for about a month so that each time I called, the topic of sorting the photos came up. It wasn't as if she had dozens of albums and even if she did, she has more than enough space to keep them as she lives in a large house. I wanted to say, 'Please don't work so hard. I'll throw them away for you', but of course I could not. I just voiced my agreement repeatedly, 'Oh, is that so? That was hard work, wasn't it?'

This kind of operation is going on constantly not only for albums but for all kinds of things like books, tableware, etc. My mother-in-law says that because she lives in a large house she has tended to keep and put away so many things. As we now have to pay for even throwing things away, she is trying to get rid of things little by little, by giving them to people or contributing to bazaars. She seems to feel sorry for her children who would have to sort out the knick-knacks after her death. As a daughter-in-law I must say I appreciate her efforts.

As it takes more than six hours by plane and train, we visit Kyushu only twice a year, in the summer and for New Year, but each time we go, the house gets neater and tidier.

Finally, the other day, the family grave became the target of her tidying up. My mother-in-law had the urns of the close relatives taken out of the grave and consigned to the ossuary of the temple. She asked the temple to dispose of the urns of the distant relatives; she then had workmen seal the grave. My mother-in-law had taken care of the grave of her husband's family for many years, and this issue was a primary concern for her. Even if she had wanted to pass the job onto the next generation, her son, my husband, working in Tokyo, could not be counted upon and as her daughter-in-law – that's me – is from Tokyo also, the possibility of our returning to Kyushu in the future was very small. She had always been concerned that she had to do something so that the grave of the ancestors would not become neglected, with no one to tend the grave. My father-in-law's illness was slowly progressing, which may have helped in speeding up this decision.

Are you tidying up the grave as well? I almost said, but I myself was not prepared to take care of the grave in Kyushu either.

'Thank you very much' was what I inadvertently said instead. But, in fact, what my mother-in-law really wants is for us to build a grave in Tokyo and bring the urns here. For the time being I have not said anything about it.

Currently the target of her tidying up process is the oil paintings she has been painting as a hobby. She is now sorting out the canvasses that have accumulated through the years. As she has been painting for almost thirty years, she has a cupboard full of paintings, and at the moment she is trying to throw away most of them. I feel that she should at least keep her own paintings.

'Please keep them. Who knows? They might become valuable posthumously like the works of Van Gogh.'

'I don't have any painting that's that good, so it's OK. Don't worry.'

My mother-in-law does not feel comfortable unless she is ready twenty minutes before departure. That is how she is, it's her nature. All I can do is look on.

TRANSLATED BY H. MIYAZAKI AND Y. TAKAHASHI

60.

The Remaining Hours

Asako Ono

****

Since my childhood I had remained unable to understand how my father's mind worked. As a daughter I did not like his occupation.

Father had been engaged in producing films for more than fifty years. His income was not stable, because his occupation was nothing more than that of a dilettante. In fact, mother was always dealing with financial crises. He produced adult films for some years. I knew he did it for a living, but I despised him for that and never talked to him during that period.

Three years ago, mother suddenly died of a heart attack. I was all the more sad, because I thought that so many years of a hard life had caused her death. I was at a loss because I was uncertain as to whether I could have a good relationship with father.

At the same time I was afraid of losing father. It was not only because I would be lonely, but because without him I would be obliged to liquidate his company, which no longer had any employees. Every troublesome matter would be left to me, his married daughter, to sort out.

The title to his plot in the cemetery and his house have been shared with his brother and sisters for half a century and nothing has been negotiated amongst them.

About the time the rainy season set in, father phoned to me, to say that he was suffering from a mild fever. I was afraid it would cause pneumonia, which would be fatal. I hurriedly took him to a hospital in the city, where he regularly had check-ups for hypertension.

Looking at the results of his blood test, Dr K, the director of the department of the circulatory organs and physician in charge of father, frowned:

'Something is wrong with the digestive organs and the liver. Let us examine them with a stomach camera.'

The doctor reserved the room for the check-up to be carried out two weeks later. I was dumbfounded when I happened to notice the words 'suspicion of cancer' on the margin of the questionnaire paper I was to take back on the day. Naturally father saw them himself. On the way back in the car he said to me: 'We have had no cancer patients in our family history. Anyway I won't undergo an operation even if an unexpected result follows.'

Although he pretended to be tough, he fell seriously ill soon after hearing the news, perhaps because of the shocking words, and he was hospitalized before the check-up day.

I expected Dr K to be in charge, but he was going to leave the hospital to open his own clinic, so in his place Dr N was to take charge of father. He came to the sickroom to greet us. He was very tall, but he was much younger than his predecessor, as young as Dr K's child. To be frank I was disappointed.

One by one Dr N carried out the scheduled examination of the heart, the stomach and the large intestine and so on by the use of echocardiography, endoscope and CT. Father by nature was nervous and stubborn. He was so self-centred as to make a complaint even about a routine intravenous drip. Dr N came to father's sickroom as often as possible and listened attentively to the old man's complaints. Soon I came to trust this young doctor.

Ten days after the hospitalization, when all the necessary data were ready for evaluation, father and I were called into the doctor's office. In the small room a number of photos were clearly displayed in the light. As soon as father sat down in the chair, he began to tell the doctor as if to take the initiative:

'Tell me the truth, sir. I am now eighty years of age. It won't be surprising if I am no more tomorrow, but, as you know, I have some things to settle before that because I am an independent businessman. There is no one to do that work in my place. That is the reason why I ask for the truth.'

Father delivered his comment in a single breath. A moment later Dr N quietly said:

'This is a photo of the stomach taken with the camera. We have taken samples of tissue of the inflamed part and carried out a biopsy. The result shows the disease is not benign.'

Dr N continued, choosing his words carefully so as not to shock the patient unnecessarily. He knew some patients were too sensitive to listen to the doctor's words.

'It has been developing there for more than ten years and now spread to the lymph glands and the liver. It is at stage four. I am sorry to say, but there is no hope of a complete recovery.'

At that moment I looked at father in profile and found him smiling gently. He asked:

'Do you mean it is too late to cure it? Do you mean it was possible to treat it if it was discovered earlier?'

'No, I do not mean that. At whatever stage it is discovered, it is the best time for a person, I think.'

He added that it was impossible to undertake an operation. The question was whether father wanted chemotherapy or not.

Father said: 'I do not want chemotherapy. All that I want is to make the best use of the remaining hours, and liquidate the company and dispose of my household goods. In the last days I wish for hospice care.'

I thought he was ready to accept the inevitable. He was going to settle all the things he should have done earlier, before his fire of life disappeared. I had a deep feeling of sympathy for him.

I remembered the words 'Japan's cancer refugees' I had read about. I was afraid that the hospital would dismiss the patient who had refused to receive medical treatment, just as some country would expel aliens unwilling to observe the domestic laws.

'Can I still stay here and be taken care of?'

'Yes, of course, you can. I will be in charge of you. A lot of people want to enter the hospice attached to the hospital – from outside, too. You had better register for the hospice care soon.'

Father did not ask the doctor how long he might survive, though he appeared to want to know.

The following day I asked Dr N that question in confidence.

'A matter of months. It depends on each individual patient, though.'

Now I think of how long father will live, even when I have a look at the numbers, '20/02/08', stamped on a jar of mayonnaise, indicating the 'best-before' date. He will be lonely and unhappy if he devotes the rest of his life only to liquidating his company. His remaining hours are the time, though brief, in which I can show filial affection for him and be a help for both the first and last time.

TRANSLATED BY S. KURAMOCHI

PART 8

LIVING ALONE REHEARSAL

61.

Living Alone Rehearsal

Yoko Yoshida

****

My husband, who is thinking about living abroad for a period of time, went to Malaysia to apply for his visa. Apparently, he went to apply for it by himself with the help of his friend who lives there. He went with a large amount of complicated paperwork. Because of something to do with the round-trip ticket, he had to stay in Malaysia for two weeks.

This was supposed to be my one-in-a-million chance. I could use all twenty-four hours for myself. I could do anything such as eating meals while watching my favourite TV shows. I could come home anytime I liked. It was all up to me to go to places like the cinema, kabuki or museums. I was perfectly free except for the 'homework' that sprang up without expectation in front of me.

The morning I saw my husband off, I cleaned and did some laundry and went shopping very quickly, thinking that otherwise I might get used to being lazy. When my husband is away sometimes, and when I only need to make meals for myself, I don't usually cook; but if it was two weeks I couldn't do that. I bought enough food for two or three days and I made *miso* soup as usual. I grilled some dried fish and I set the table with homemade pickles that I always have in the house.

The 'homework' I mentioned above was a new experience. It was to make a one-and-a-half-hour speech about an essay and deliver the speech in front of an audience. This is one of the things that we do in the essay group that I belong to. It was my turn this time and it's the thing I don't do well. But I couldn't refuse, saying, 'I can't possibly do it'. The pressure on me became greater and greater. (What should I do? What should I talk about?) I thought about it all the time, putting a heavy weight on my heart. And what's more, the day of the speech was two days before my husband was due home. I wouldn't be able to enjoy my freedom as much as I would want. Although I was worried, I chose to take a positive attitude. It was no use trying to be more than I am. I had to show my true self.

By the way, at this time, I started exchanging e-mails with my husband for the first time. I felt strange reading my husband's e-mails which started out with, 'Dear Yoko'. He wrote to say that he had arrived safely, was supported by his friends and that he was enjoying his life.

I also replied to him. 'Dear Hiroshi', I wrote, 'I am very uneasy thinking about a big earthquake coming while you are away. But I have the homework. It looks like time will fly . . .'

Let me get back to the preparation of the speech homework. After preparing my introduction, I tried to write out a draft. After making a rough draft, I started practising speaking while timing the presentation. But the work didn't proceed smoothly. Every time I realized I should add some lines, I added and rewrote. I kept doing things like that and at end, time was running out. When I finished preparing the speech, it was the day before I had to give it. I felt while I was working that it was exactly the same as writing an essay. 'What do I want to convey? There need to be examples. Draw the theme close to yourself. Keep writing and the essay will wrap itself around the theme.' In the end, the title that I wasn't even thinking about came to mind. It was: 'How Writing Essays Changed Me'.

Nevertheless, I was grateful for the situation where I only had to concentrate on what I was doing without preparing meals for my husband. On the day of the speech, although I delivered it with passion, it ended forty minutes before it was supposed to. I couldn't do anything but start a discussion. Many people had opinions in response to the first point put forward and it became a very lively and friendly atmosphere that saved me.

I was relieved of the burden I had been carrying and for the two days before my husband returned home I enjoyed lunch and dinner with my friends.

From next year, my husband is going to start his long-term stay abroad. I declared that I wanted my anchor to remain in Japan and that I would be staying here. Although my husband couldn't possibly have imagined this outcome, for the first time since we got married, I said 'No' to him.

I am secretly looking forward to living alone. I am sorry, my dear.

TRANSLATED BY P. HALTMAN

62.

An Occasional Get-away Trip

Kyoko Amano

****

On some days I have no appointments with anyone but actually do have a lot of things to deal with. But of course those things can wait until the following day. On a day like that, for no special reason, I sometimes feel like going out alone. On that particular morning, too, I woke up, took out the rubbish and when I heard the weather forecast saying, 'It's going to be a fine day today although we are in the middle of the rainy season', I suddenly decided to go out. When I feel like this, I quickly put on some make-up and throw on some casual clothes. Putting my purse and a magazine for reading on the train in my backpack, I call out, 'I'll be going out for a while' to my husband who is still in bed and I'm ready to set out.

My destination is almost always the same. It's the ancient city of Kamakura which I can reach in about an hour and half by train from the nearest station. In fact, it doesn't have to be Kamakura, but as I can go there directly without changing trains, it's an ideal place for this kind of brief and simple getaway trip.

Many years ago, a well-known woman marathon runner who lives in my prefecture disappeared for a few days and caused a commotion. 'I wanted to go somewhere far away. I jumped on the train and the next thing I knew, I found myself in Kamakura, looking at the sea.'

I remember she was making a comment like this on TV after her disappearance. Whenever I get on this train heading for Kamakura for my get-away, I remember this comment and I can't help chuckling. 'Yeah, I now understand how you must have been feeling. Even an "ordinary person" like me feels like escaping from everyday life once in a while for no particular reason.'

Recently my itinerary for the get-away trip is more or less fixed. When I get to Kamakura station, I pop into a convenience store and buy some rice balls, a bottle of Japanese tea and a bottle of sports drink and get on a bus. The bus takes me to the starting point of the hiking route that I like to take.

When I was young, Kamakura was a town where I would walk down Komachi Street with my girlfriends, all dressed up, or eat in restaurants mentioned in magazines specializing in gourmet dishes, or admire flowers in the quiet temple gardens. For me it was a town with an atmosphere of luxury and calmness. I also have romantic memories of walking along the beach admiring the sunset. But now, for me, it's a town where I can spend the day as I like, completely on my own, not caring how I am dressed, without being bothered by anyone.

When I got off the bus, the sun was blazing. I pulled my hat down low to keep the sun away and wore sunglasses. This made me feel as if I were on some furtive mission and trying to avoid people's eyes. It is true that, as it was a get-away trip after all, I didn't want to bump into people I knew.

I walked under the scorching sun for a while until I reached the path I was heading for. As soon as I reached the pathway that was so narrow it could be easily missed, it was as if I'd stepped into another world, with dense cedar trees lining the mountain path. No one was there. Enjoying the occasional cool breeze, I walked slowly, taking off my hat and sunglasses. I first learned of this hiking route when I visited Kamakura with a group of friends living in the same condominium building. I realized that the natural world around Kamakura was as appealing as fashionable Kamakura itself, and since then, this had become my favourite place.

After a walk of forty to fifty minutes, I reached a scenic rest stop. On the way, I passed several hikers but there were fewer hikers here than usual, considering it was a weekend. It was lunch time and I was beginning to get hungry so I sat down in the shade and munched on the rice balls I had bought at the convenience store. My husband would also be eating at home by now, possibly something a little tastier. He retired a year ago and since then he has learned to get himself something to eat if I'm not there. As I often go out anyway, he wouldn't have found it strange that I left the house abruptly early in the morning.

Feeling a little refreshed, I resumed my walk and went on further up the mountain path. When I climbed to a scenic lookout on top of a small hill, I found a big fat cat sitting on a bench and sat down next to him. I could see the coastline of Yuigahama Beach far away. 'I took the children there for a swim several times, didn't I?' I said to the cat, tickling his throat. The cat narrowed his eyes contentedly. I realized that besides greeting the other hikers with a 'Hello', this conversation with the cat was the first conversation I had that day. I played with the cat for a while, drinking my sports drink, and then left the lookout, bidding the cat farewell.

From there onwards, the path went downwards and my get-away trip was nearing its end. I descended a long flight of stairs that soon appeared and reached the garden of the temple renowned for its Zen Training Hall. The sun was still beating down on the stone pavement. I took out my hat and sunglasses from my backpack again. This temple is always full of worshippers and tourists. When you have been walking along the mountain path alone, the heat and crowd combined can suddenly make you feel exhausted. With a sideways glance at the groups taking photos of each other in front of the temple bell, I hurried out of the main gate. From there, I headed straight for Kitakamakura station.

I always finish off my get-away trip with coffee and cake. As soon as I entered the small coffee shop in front of the station, I felt my perspiration drying up. A natural breeze is wonderful, of course, but the breeze from the air conditioner wasn't bad either.

From about this point, I start feeling myself being pulled back to my everyday life. As I left the house in a hurry, I hadn't had any coffee this morning. The hot coffee, the first coffee of the day, tasted especially good. The sweet cake helped sooth my tired limbs.

Outside the window, I could see crowds of people trying to get on the train, all carrying bags filled with souvenirs. Yes, that's a good idea. I'll buy the dove-shaped sable biscuits that are a Kamakura specialty for my husband. It's a bit strange to be buying souvenirs on a get-away trip, but that's how my trips always end up. I was already planning the dinner: 'If I get on the train now, I'll have plenty of time to make a Japanese-style beef and potato stew.' Sitting in the seat by the window, feeling the movement of the train, I found myself planning my schedule for the next day, down to the last detail.

TRANSLATED BY H. MIYAZAKI AND Y. TAKAHASHI

63.

'The Assistant Driver's Seat'

Fumi Ishii

****

My eldest son invited me to spend Christmas at his home.

I was told that his wife would prepare salad and hors d'oeuvres and make Osaka-style pressed sushi. I was to cook chicken for the main course. I took my time and made thorough preparations. I carefully stuffed the fowl and roasted it well; I also tied a red and green ribbon round it so as to create the atmosphere of Christmas.

At six o'clock my son came to my house to pick me up. I held the plate of chicken firmly in my hands and sat beside the driver.

'Fasten your seat belt,' said my son. I was absent-minded.

'How can I fasten it if I am holding the plate with both hands?' I retorted. My son extended his arm round me and fastened the belt for me.

It would take a quarter of an hour to reach his house, and I had a lot of things to talk about on the way. Usually, there are few opportunities to talk with him. I felt I would burst if I didn't talk. I felt like talking about his business or about my grandchild's entrance examination. But I didn't know how to break the ice about the topic. I just had too much on my mind to talk about in such a short time. While I kept silent, I began to feel myself more relaxed. As I sat comfortably beside my son, time went by.

My eldest son's house is in a new residential area where smart houses stand in a row. Decorative illuminations are not only fixed to the houses but also to the fences. The street, which is lined with these houses, is called 'Christmas Street', and attracts so many visitors that sometimes there are traffic jams. My son suggested that we should have a look round the area to enjoy the sights. We reached his house before we could talk about what I had in mind.

Everything was the same on the way home. I knew I would have no time to have a conversation with my son if I missed this chance. I wanted to ask him if his business was going well; if he was overworking; if Kota, my grandchild, was working hard at school? I also wanted to urge him to stop smoking. Those were all his private problems in which I could not interfere. I had no idea which I should talk about first. Then I realized that I should make the most of the brief time we had together. However, despite my wish that the time would last longer, our car soon reached my house, and my son opened the door for me.

'Thank you very much. Drive carefully on your way home,' I said.

He saluted me by raising his hand. His car made a U-turn and went off.

A few days later, I went shopping in a store near my house. A couple I had seldom seen entered the lift I was in. After exchanging greetings with them, I went out into the street. The couple seemed to have headed for the car park at the back of the store. I think they were in their fifties. They must have been shopping in preparation for the New Year. In the car the husband must have been in the driver's seat and the wife in the seat beside him; the Japanese usually call the seat beside the driver's 'the assistant driver's seat'. A couple sitting in the front seat of a car must be a very common sight, but I could not help feeling jealous of them. While walking to the supermarket, I kept imaging that particular scene.

Then it occurred to me that I hadn't sat in the 'assistant driver's seat' for more than fifteen years. The memory of the Christmas Day came back to my mind. On that day I sat in the 'assistant driver's seat' beside my son – an experience I had not had for a long time. In my son's car, his wife usually sat in that seat and I sat in the back seat with my grandchildren.

Whenever I was in the car with my husband, my usual seat of course was the 'assistant driver's seat'. When my children were very young, they were quite lively in the back seat. During the summer holidays, my three children were always in the back seat and I never failed to sit beside my husband. The 'assistant driver's seat' is a place for a wife and for a mother, too. My children remained quiet while they had something to eat or were given some sweets, but they would soon begin to quarrel. Sometimes, one or more of them would get car-sick. This meant we had to stop the car at the side of the road, and I had to do my duty as a mother. I would give them a vinyl bag I carried with me, or take out a wet towel from my bag.

Those happy old days did not last long. As I look back, my memory gradually fades. My eldest son married after he graduated from university. My second son established himself in business and left home after his graduation. My daughter became a college student. I should have felt happy to see my children begin to rely on themselves, but the fact was that I felt depressed every day; my energy just disappeared. I heard of the 'being gone' syndrome afterwards. I was in a void; whatever I tried to do, I felt myself falling into the bowels of the earth.

In those days my husband was still at work in an office. In the evening at weekends he would say after we finished dinner:

'Let's go for a drive.'

I would nod. Opening the door of the car, I seated myself deep in the 'assistant driver's seat'. We had no definite destination. We just drove around our residential area for about half an hour. Most of the houses were new and had the lights on and all the families were enjoying their own lives. Seeing this made me feel more at ease.

My husband said nothing during the drive and I felt entirely comfortable sitting next to him. The little space in our car was filled with peace of mind. After a life of exerting myself as a wife and mother, I felt quite at ease now. A year later, my spirits improved considerably.

Now my husband is dead, and I have no chance to sit in the 'assistant driver's seat'. But I can't let go of my attachment to the seat. I have become accustomed to my present situation, but I sometimes miss sitting in that seat.

My daughter, now married, is concerned about me living alone, and takes me out in her car for lunch or shopping. When I am about to get into the back seat, she will say:

'The Assistant Driver's Seat'

'This is not a taxi. Why don't you sit in the "assistant driver's seat"?'

I smile a bitter smile and sit beside her. That seat is not my usual one, but sitting in an 'assistant driver's seat' gives me a pleasant feeling.

TRANSLATED BY N. KUMABE

64.

The Red-hot Kettle

Yoko Kishita

****

I had been thinking of upgrading some of our kitchen appliances to make life a bit easier for the two of us–an elderly couple; but for some reason or other I had delayed doing so.

It was in early October and an unusually cold day; but on returning home I found it was unexpectedly warm inside.

'It is very cold this evening. I've got the kettle on,' said my husband, who did not usually do any housework.

When I opened the door to the kitchen, however, I found it was surprisingly warm. I saw a red, round thing floating in the darkness.

'What is that? Is that a human soul I have often heard about? Quite unbelievable.'

After a moment I realized it was the kettle we use every day. I switched on the light. Sure enough I found the stainless-steel kettle was red-hot, as if it was going to melt, still on the burning gas hob. The water was gone. I was relieved to find it in time. If I had returned home any later, what would have happened? The mere thought made me shiver.

My husband said, nonchalantly:

'I forgot about it.'

I felt all the more surprised because he seemed indifferent.

Then and there I decided to buy a new type of gas hob with a safety cut-out device which would automatically switch off after the selected time had elapsed.

I collected catalogues and started looking round show-rooms.

I learned that most of the safety devices were programmed to cut out after two hours, but a period of two hours was too long. The kettle would become red-hot well before two hours had elapsed. I wanted a type with a device which would cut out in a much shorter time. Finally, I found the type of burner I was looking for. It was one integrated into a system-kitchen. The timer could be set at ten-minute intervals between thirty minutes and 120 minutes.

I decided to buy a system kitchen. It cost about 1,200,000 yen. I decided to remodel the kitchen, which would include an underfloor heating system. I arranged with the gas company to remodel the whole kitchen, as I learned that it would do the remodelling as part of the package. As a result I had to take out all the household goods from the kitchen.

'This is a nuisance, as you know,' I said.

'Every one says so. If you like, I will help you.'

The staff member in charge made the offer, but I thought I as a housewife I was the only person who could decide what to keep and what to throw away. Being a housewife for the past fifty years, I was responsible for taking care of the household goods, so naturally I would not leave the selection to others.

I insisted on dealing with it myself, but I was at a loss. There were too many things to make decisions about: the flood of gifts and other things coming from seven cupboards on the walls.

'You can throw them all away. Almost everything is unnecessary. Don't be nostalgic, Mum.'

My daughter, who was living next door, said to me coolly, and made no offer of help.

Once the remodelling started, everything went smoothly according to schedule. The old sink was carried away and the tiles on the walls were removed quickly, but it took a week for the floor to be replaced and to have the electrical points in place ready for use.

First of all, I set the timer. I set it at thirty minutes, instead of 120 minutes, which was its default setting. This was the very function I aimed at when I decided to buy a new system kitchen. Within thirty minutes the kettle would not get red-hot, even if we forgot to turn off the gas. We could cook meals within this period.

However, there was one unexpected drawback. The function did not work properly for a metal fibre mat, which I often used to cook stews. I could save gas energy by using it. When I cooked black soybeans towards the end of last year, I used the mat. After a short time, I heard the digital voice announcement: 'The safety stop cut-out device will be activated.' Immediately after that the burner cut out automatically.

Even if there is some inconvenience, safety is the top priority in my home. Due to the underfloor heating, it is very warm inside, so we have spent the New Year season comfortably.

My husband goes out twice a month to play *go* with friends. Recently he started going out on Fridays, when I also go out. I do not know why. Perhaps because he does not want to stay at home alone. The traumatic image of the red-hot kettle still remains in his mind's eye, although he pretends to be indifferent to the incident.

TRANSLATED BY S. KURAMOCHI

65.

My Husband is Cooking

Kyoko Amano

****

As soon as I arrived home and opened the front door, I was greeted by the flavour of soy sauce mixed with sweet rice wine wafting about in the hall. This is it. This is what I have been dreaming of.

Instead of saying, 'I'm home', I said, 'Smells good!' and took off my coat. I could see my husband in the kitchen wearing an apron, struggling with a frying pan in one hand. I walked by the kitchen, glancing in his direction out of the corner of my eye, and took my time changing into my house clothes. When I came back, broiled sardines and hot salad were on the table.

I was chatting with my friends once when the topic of getting along with your husband after his retirement came up. We all wanted our husbands to cook. This was a wish we all shared. 'Won't it be wonderful to find dinner ready when we come home?' Not satisfied with that, one friend even said: 'Just once, I'd like to call home just about the time dinner is all ready and say, "I don't need dinner tonight".' We got quite excited saying this would be paying back for our plight all these years and imagined how much of a kick we'd get out of it. But in the end, we came to the conclusion that it would be a waste of all the ingredients and we couldn't possibly do that. We were housewives all right.

I told my husband of this conversation partly as a joke. I don't know if this was one of the reasons but last autumn, my husband suddenly began to go to a 'cooking class for men over sixty'. His very commendable motive seemed to be his desire to manage his own diet. My husband is slightly diabetic and has some dietary restrictions. The dishes taught in his cooking class were mainly fish recipes and other healthy dishes, and the calories were all calculated as well. It was just what one would expect of a cooking class for senior citizens.

So eight years after retirement, my husband has started to work in the kitchen, although the occasions are still few and far between. As a wife this should be a very welcome state of affairs but . . .

As my husband always wants to begin everything by fully equipping himself, he is not satisfied with the old pots and pans at home. He wants to have the same utensils as the ones used in the cooking class. Even with something like measuring spoons, he doesn't trust the measuring spoon that I've been using for years. A blunt knife is of course out of the question.

I'd like to complain, 'Why don't you use what we have at home?' but he might then say, 'Well, then, I won't do any more cooking.' I don't want that to happen, either. So thanks to my husband's cooking, we have an array of new cooking utensils.

What makes me secretly grind my teeth, though, is the way he tries to follow the recipe, word for word. If the recipe calls for one level tablespoon of sugar, it has to be really one level tablespoon, exactly. If there is a dent or a little bump on the surface of the sugar, he will try again and again until it is exactly one level tablespoon, no more, no less. If the recipe says, 'Sprinkle some minced chives on top', chives they must be. Substituting with green onions is unthinkable. I don't say a word. 'Patience, Patience!' What a lot of patience one needs to keep one's husband cooking happily!

'Isn't this a little too spicy?'

'No, it's just right.'

'I overcooked it and it has become too dry.'

'Oh, I think it tastes just fine like this.'

Whether it's too hot or all dried up, I have nothing but words of praise.

After a little while, either because he has got used to cooking or because he has learned to cut corners, he is now a bit more relaxed.

'It says use pork but there's some ham in the fridge, so I'll use that instead,' he'd say. He has also begun to show interest in recipes other than the ones he learned in his cooking class. He bought a book, *Easy Recipes for the Microwave Oven*, and he is enjoying trying those recipes almost as if they were some kind of experiment. When he started, making one dish was the best he could do, but he can now produce two dishes for one meal.

I wish he would also do the washing up, but he is exhausted after cooking a meal and I don't want to become too 'indebted' to him either, so it may be just as well.

Our sons, who come home from time to time, seem worried about the change in their father. 'What's come over Dad? Is his time nearly up or something?'

I am worried, too, but in a different way. My husband is always quick to get excited about something but just as quick to cool down. There have been several instances like that in the past.

It is now time to pay the tuition for the new term's cooking class.

'Have you registered for the new class?'

'No, not yet.'

'Oh, you'd better hurry or you'll miss registration.'

My husband went to register the next day, but is it just my imagination that he seemed just a little reluctant?

TRANSLATED BY H. MIYAZAKI AND Y. TAKAHASHI

66.

Roses

Mitsuo Urata

****

'Your wife is so wonderful! She does the housework, takes care of the children and of course she is a very efficient worker. And on top of all that, she even grows roses!'

My colleague's wife who visiting our house was full of admiration. I detected a hint of envy. She was implying that I was a lucky man to have such a wonderful wife.

I was at a loss for words. So my wife does the housework and takes care of the children? Really!

Who does the laundry and the cleaning? And who gives the children a bath and takes them to the nursery and picks them up? And who, may I ask, puts them to bed and reads them stories at night!

In those days (and maybe even today), the housework and looking after the children were considered to be the wife's job even when both husband and wife worked full-time. Our arrangement was special. So even if we were misunderstood or not understood at all, I thought that it couldn't be helped as I knew we were the ones going against the norm. I was reconciled to that.

But my wife is growing roses, too? Now what could that mean?

There's the matter of winter dressing, then from early spring, insect pest control, pruning and weeding, and when the buds begin to appear, removing the superfluous ones. All these chores take time and effort, and roses demand special care and attention. Who on earth has been doing all this?

Papa Meilland, Queen Elizabeth, Princess Michiko, White Christmas, Blue Moon, Peace, etc. Now who taught all these names to my wife, who didn't know a single name of any rose?

'Are you going round telling your colleagues at work that you are growing roses?' I couldn't keep the roughness out of my voice.

'Oh, I'm not saying anything. She just misunderstood, I suppose.' My wife shrugged off my remarks.

'Well, if that's the case, you'd better tell her that I am the one who is growing the roses!'

'I'll do that.' But by her tone I knew she was saying, 'Don't be bothered by such trifles.'

It happened like this one morning.

'Can I take some of these roses to the office?'

It was just before I was leaving for work and I was very busy. My wife was calling me from the garden. She wasn't asking for my permission. She was just notifying me, as usual. But if I left her to do it herself, I was afraid anything could happen.

'What? It's OK but be sure to cut them just below the five-leaflet leaf.'

'What's a five-leaflet leaf?'

'Oh, I'll come and do it.'

I went out into the garden with my tie still half-tied and cut some splendid roses that my wife pointed out. While I was at it, I removed the thorns with my pruning scissors and wrapped the roses up in a newspaper and handed her the bouquet.

'Everyone was so surprised. They thought the roses were magnificent,' my wife told me when she came home. I had always thought that they were words of praise for me and my roses before I heard the words of her colleague from the NHS office.

Since then, every year, when the roses begin to bloom in early May, my wife would cut them and, beaming with pleasure, take them to her office and put them on her desk.

Years have passed.

My wife became ill, left her job before retirement and passed away.

I had already stopped growing roses. One by one, the untended rose shrubs withered away.

Only one rose shrub called 'Peace', described in the brochure as 'robust, big flowers, blooms well', survived. When the season comes around, a cream-coloured rose that is no longer so big blooms all alone at the end of a spindly branch.

The rose that no one cuts any more sheds its petals at the end of the branch.

TRANSLATED BY H. MIYAZAKI AND Y. TAKAHASHI

67.

Shall We Dance?

Mitsuo Urata

****

My reflexes are slow and I have never been a good athlete. When I was at primary school, I always came last in races. I couldn't do any of the things Japanese children are required to do in PE classes, like jumping over vaulting horses or doing the forward upward circling on the horizontal bar. I couldn't swim. I couldn't ride a bicycle either. Around the time I began to work, baseball was all the rage and baseball games were often organized between different sections of the company. All young men were recruited for these games, but I was always a bench-warmer.

Eventually, as I went up the corporate ladder, I could not get away from playing golf. When you become a departmental head, golf becomes part of your job requirement. It is how you associate with people both inside and outside the company. Despite my efforts, I continued to hit sixty to seventy strokes for half a round. I did not want to become a burden to my golf companions, so I decided to make an extra effort. My wife, who was afraid of becoming a golf widow, observed my efforts with an icy look. I worked out a plan. I kept a set of clubs at the driving range and went there directly from the office. I hit 100 to 150 balls and then went home, as if I had come straight from work. After continuing this clandestine practice for a year, my golf improved somewhat. Although I had started to play golf because I needed to for my job, I began to enjoy it. My high school and junior high school classmates were organizing golf competitions several times a year and I decided to participate in them. My friends were surprised that I played golf at all. The system of handicaps in golf gives you a chance to win even if you are a poor player. Given the maximum handicap of 36, I won my first competition. When you win, your handicap is lowered by 30 per cent, so my next handicap was 25. This prompted one of the old bullies with a sharp tongue to say: 'This is going to be your first and last win!' To get back at him, I continued my clandestine practice and won again the next time. My handicap went down to 17. As might be expected, I have not won since, but I now enjoy playing golf like everyone else.

It was more than thirty years ago when my wife, who had been carefully scrutinizing the bulletin from the city hall, looked up and said, 'They're advertising a dance class for beginners. Let's join.' When she was a student, my wife had learned to dance as a part of the PE curriculum. I had not taken any notice of dancing, considering it an activity for weaklings, but I thought it would be fun to dance with my wife and I knew it wouldn't bode well for me if I were to go against her wishes. After work, we both went to the community hall where the dance class was to be held. Only a few men were there, just as I had expected, but to my surprise I was the only true beginner. All the others had enjoyed dancing when they were young and had come to the class to revive their now rusty skills. The lady instructor first explained the steps on the blackboard. We then did some shadow dancing and proceeded to dance with a partner. The instructress took charge of me, the true beginner. It was the first time for me to hold a woman other than my wife, one hand at her back and the other hand holding her hand. We were standing so close that we could feel each other's breath. It was difficult to keep calm to start with. I was supposed to do my steps following the voice of the instructress calling out, 'one, two and three'. But maybe because of my slow reflexes, it took a second or two for the command from my brain to travel through my nervous system and reach my feet. As a result, I would step back when I should have stepped forward and step forward when I should have been stepping back. My chest would bump into my instructress' bosom. One day, when I had not made any progress after a number of lessons, she said, 'Do make a serious effort, would you?' I detected a note of anger in her voice. After returning home that night, I told my wife that I was going to finish dancing. She seemed disappointed.

Shall We Dance?

My wife had a best friend who was a full-time homemaker and loved to dance. After my wife was invited to a performance by her dancing school, she decided to go to the dancing school herself. But an extra activity on top of her work, housework and taking care of the children, was doomed to be short-lived. Many years after this, when she retired from work due to a brain hemorrhage, she started taking hula lessons as a form of rehabilitation. She certainly loved to dance.

One night many years after my wife's death, I watched the film *Shall We Dance?* on TV. Although his motives were somewhat questionable, a drab middle-aged man tries hard to learn to dance, without telling his wife, and finally succeeds. After seeing the film, I suddenly realized something.

As my wife and I both worked, I helped with the household chores and taking care of the children a great deal more than most men of my generation. My wife's friends, envious of my wife, were full of praise. 'How kind your husband is!' In fact, I was conceited enough to be in total agreement with them. But the middle-aged hero in the film, who does not appear to be so athletic, realizes his dream of mastering dancing. If I had put into dancing the same zeal I had put into golf, I would have been able to master dancing, too, athletic or not. Although it would have been impossible for me to dance gracefully with elegant steps, I would have reached the level where I could enjoy dancing with my wife. Although I did not hesitate to make a great effort for something I was interested in, I did not make this effort for my wife. If, at the time, I had secretly continued to learn dancing and had invited her to dance at our wedding anniversary, I am sure she would have been delighted and would have beamed with pleasure. I need not have been as self-sacrificing as the couple in the 'Gift of the Magi'. I just needed to care a little and try to please my wife. Far from being the kind person I thought I was, I realized I was a very cold person at heart. I was dumbfounded.

It is now too late.

TRANSLATED BY H. MIYAZAKI AND Y. TAKAHASHI

68.

Warm Winter Sunlight

Keiko Takano

****

Early in the afternoon, I went out for a walk in the warm winter sunlight. I usually walk as far as a small park at the end of our residential street.

I had had two operations on my leg, and I am now able to walk again. I walked slowly with a stick in my hand.

The park was quiet. I heard neither the noise of a car nor a human voice. Strange to relate, I felt quite relaxed as if I were in my own secret place.

The park boasts a solitary old bench. It welcomes me gently in the sun. I remain seated on the bench for a while; after looking up at the sky, I consider the various trees around the park and enjoy this small natural environment exercising my five senses to the full. I take deep breaths and rid myself of the rubbish that has accumulated in my mind.

The yellow leaves of ginkgo trees in late autumn are especially beautiful. They increase in brilliancy as if they are unwilling to let go of autumn. In winter, the leaves are blown away and they become bare. They stand there extending their branches straight as if to pierce the sky. This scene prompts me to consider what life is all about and encourages me with positive thoughts when I feel in a complaining mood.

This year I reached seventy. 'The seventieth year' makes me realize that I am in the last chapter of life. When I look back at my past life, I regret how it has been marked by much sorrow and distress, although it has also enjoyed many pleasures.

I have sometimes been hurt, but equally I must have hurt others unintentionally. When I think of those things, the realization of my being immature as a human being touches me to the core.

I really want to make as much as I can of the days ahead; I very much want to keep in touch with all those connected with me.

I had a hard time in my sixties. The time passed by as harshly as a spring storm, which is a sympton that winter is over and spring is coming.

I had a disease in my joints before I was aware of it. I had to endure the pain for a long time and grew uneasy, thinking that I would have to deal with the implications of having an operation. Impatience and sorrow attacked me alternately, and caused further injury within me. All I could do was to accept the reality, albeit against my will.

A year has since passed. I am grateful now for my daily life free from any pain. I feel I have completed the ascent of a long slope.

I remember something a certain actor said, although I am not sure when I first heard it. He advises that those who have some mental or physical problem and can find no place to live in the great outdoors should simply look up at the sky. He says that the sky is that part of nature which is closest to us; when we reflect on the endless great universe, our distress and sorrow seem as miniscule as dust. The actor leads a busy life, but he feels refreshed when he looks up at the sky while jogging early in the morning.

Now I cannot walk about freely without the help of a stick, but I feel somewhat relieved by the sky, which accepts everyone equally.

I hear an aeroplane buzzing overhead. I look up and see its diaphanous airframe moving, as if it were melting into the infinitely deep blue sky. I wonder what destination the plane is heading for.

The moment I think that an aeroplane prompts us to dream, I feel a warm wind of hope blowing within me.

My house is situated in a quiet town on the outskirts of Tokyo, and it will be the last house in my life. But I cannot tell what will happen in the future. That is how life ticks along.

While I indulge in idle speculation, I see everything around me tinged faintly pink showing signs of a warm spring.

TRANSLATED BY N. KUMABE

69.

So that We Can Live to be a Hundred

Chizuko Bando

****

At 6.15 in the morning, I meet with my friend and neighbour in front of my house to start out on our morning walk. In ten minutes or so we reach the entrance of Hikarigaoka Park, then through the park to the usual place, where we are greeted with the words, 'Good morning, everyone. We wish you another good day', blaring out from the portable radios of the people standing here and there. This is followed by the familiar music of the first radio gymnastic exercise, and with the rhythmical call of 'One and two, one and two', we're off doing our gymnastic exercise. This is something we first learned at primary school and have kept on doing through junior and senior high school, right up to the present. Soon the second radio gymnastic exercise comes to an end. Around fifty to sixty people are gathered here in front of the track and field stadium today. I'd like to say that the participants are of all ages, young and old, but, in fact, they are all, without exception, middle-aged or older. The old man who is always one beat behind and the woman who jumps up and down for every move are all familiar faces. When the exercise ends, we nod to each other and disperse, all going our own way. Some people continue to walk like us while a group stays put and starts *Tai chi chuan*, or internal Chinese martial art.

The total population of Japan is about 128 million, of which twenty-six million are sixty-five years of age and older. This is approximately 20% of the total population, so it means that one in five is an old person. In fact, more and more households around us consist of aged people living on their own, including ourselves.

When he turned sixty-five last year, my husband registered at the College for Senior Citizens sponsored by Nerima ward, where we live. He said he was surprised by the wide variety of courses on offer, including 'A journey along the Silk Road' and 'Learning about therapy dogs', and by the enthusiasm of the participants. As an extension programme, an English conversation course was offered and I attended this in my husband's place. The five students, including two women who were over seventy, all shared a very positive attitude about everything. At times we surrounded our Tanzanian teacher and bombarded him with questions in our halting English. What was most surprising for me was that the gentleman who only looked about seventy-five at most was actually eighty-eight years old. He told me that he drives to the community centre himself.

I recall a scene I witnessed recently in a restaurant one afternoon. Two elderly ladies came in and sat down. Two middle-sized jugs of beer were soon served. They were drinking beer as if it were the most natural thing in the world. They chatted happily, obviously enjoying their lunch. All these elderly people must be very healthy, both in body and mind. They'll probably keep on going another five, ten or even twenty years? I have powerful role models all around me.

Here is a wonderful poem which came over the radio:

So that you can die tomorrow,
So that you can live to be a hundred,
Let's live with this in mind.
  Go ahead and see anyone you want to see
  Go ahead and eat anything you want to eat
  Go ahead and go anywhere you want to go
So that you can die tomorrow,
So that you can live to be a hundred,
Let's live with this in mind.

TRANSLATED BY H. MIYAZAKI AND Y. TAKAHASHI

70

Writing Essays for Thirty Years

Harumi Kimura

****

A letter from Mrs W said:

'Now that I have reached the age of eighty, I should like to publish at my own expense what I have scribbled down over the years. The publication could be a companion on my journey to the nether world. Would you write a foreword for it?'

She is one of those who has been attending my essay-writing class for years. When I read her work for the first time about thirty years ago, I felt as if I were the student taking down lecture notes from Mrs W; a case of putting the cart before the horse, as it were. Her ability had attained a level where her work hardly needed any correction at all. Even so, she has never once missed my monthly class and handed in her work.

Mrs W is a landlady and comes from a good old family in Tama in the suburbs of Tokyo. She used to be a major landowner but had her farmland confiscated as a result of the agrarian reforms carried out by the American GHQ soon after the Second World War. With the changing times, the land around her was rapidly turned into housing lots, and she was aware, too, of the changing rural scenery along with changes in people's attitudes and expectations. She continued to write about those changes with a calm, light touch: she even wrote how the flowers bloomed and how the trees grew rampant in a different way each year. Whatever changes took place in her surroundings, she herself has remained unchanged. Her rich literary heritage, her shy and elegant personality, her ability to write essays that arouse envy and sympathy in her readers, and her tender sensitivity have always generated pleasure and positivity among her friends in the class. When she describes plums in bloom and beech trees in bud, her writing is not a mere description of the changes of the seasons but is accompanied by incisive observations about society and civilization, which projects a sense of the profound. Mrs W is never too officious, and you come to respect her as someone who is undoubtedly descended from an ancient and noble family.

The students attending my class hand in their drafts beforehand. All the manuscripts are copied in a reduced size at the office and bound up as a single volume, a copy of which is then given to every student. In class, the students take it in turn to read out their own essay. All the students then sympathetically discuss the work and offer a critique of its merits with a view to perfecting the composition.

The bound volume usually contains sixteen or seventeen essays. Mrs W, I am told, carefully preserves all the texts that have been used in the class so far. This proves how much she loves essays, although she does have the advantage of owning a storehouse (well built with thick mortar) where she keeps the texts.

In an essay, the writer should always be at the centre. When he writes about current events and gives his opinion on them, or even when he offers some information about a certain person, he should start with his own awareness of the issue. When he writes about his personal life, with himself or his family as the main characters, he may offer his views about the world but at the same time taking care to maintain his privacy; but his main objective is the ingenuity he brings to the way he expresses himself. Thus, for the writer of an essay, it is the writer himself or a particular aspect of his life that is the main focus. In my monthly class, as already mentioned, the students read their essays out loud and in so doing they reveal themselves. As a result, the texts no longer seem to be mere copied compositions but spring into life, giving us a sense of the real world inhabited by their writers. Quite a few students who have attended my essay-writing classes have since died of cancer or cerebral hemorrhage. Their life and opinions, the proof that they have lived in the world, now exist nowhere but in Mrs W's storehouse. I must say, it is wonderful that Mrs W is preserving those things, or indeed those people.

About a year ago, Mrs W said to me in a somewhat bashful manner:

'I haven't handed in my essay, because I couldn't write one this month. This is the first time that I have failed to do so.'

'Oh, I see,' I replied casually as I smiled back. But I should have been more aware of the significance of what Mrs W was saying to me.

Mrs W must have imposed on herself the task of writing essays as her great life-long work. On reflection, therefore, you can really imagine how distressed she was when one day she found herself unable to write. As you advance in your age, both your physical and mental strength declines, and the day will come when you are unable to write an essay.

Since that time, Mrs W has often absented herself from the class; sometimes because it was too hot or too cold; other times because one of her friends of the same age happened to die suddenly. Last summer I myself nearly fainted because of the heat coming up from the pavement.

In October, as the leaves of the maple trees began to be tinged with scarlet, I was staying in a cabin on Mt Asama, enjoying the wonderful mountain scenery, soaked in the autumnal air. The view was so fresh that it made me wonder whether I had actually recovered my eyesight. It was then that I received a letter from Mrs W, which, as I noted at the beginning, said that she was going to publish the third volume of her essays. The publication, no doubt rich in content and well produced, is something I am looking forward to receiving in the near future. I am happy to know that Mrs W continues to communicate her thoughts and messages through her essays.

I am in charge of three classes, and it is certainly the case that I have enjoyed the company of some of my students for more than thirty years. Now I have a number of successors who have acquired the ability to write essays. Some of them have established their own classes and give lectures to their students. Yet, all of them continue to attend my class and pay for their tuition. Behind their attitude to continue writing essays throughout their life is the sense of a tradition which is peculiar to the cultural life of Japanese society. In Japan, we have maintained the system of licensing the teaching of Japanese art since the Edo Period. In fact, most martial arts and artistic skills continue to be taught through this feudalistic system which is based on our vertical society. For example, in the field of tea ceremony, the art of flower arrangement, Japanese fencing (kendo) and sumo wrestling, talent has been nurtured through this traditional system, despite the fact that the vertical society has been subject to some modernization. Japanese cultural traditions still tend to be inherited, and martial arts continue to have clear lines of succession. In learning an art, great value is set on the relationship between teacher and student or that within a company. The old Japanese system of licensing is based on such relationships.

I am a lecturer at a centre of culture, but I am not in the position of being the head of a licensing system. Even so, I have come to recognize that my mission is to consolidate a group that has lasted for such a long time. When we write about personal matters in an essay, we naturally reflect the Japanese mind-set in the work. As we take time in refining our compositions, we naturally hope that more and more people will read the work and we also hope that our family and friends will remember it since it proves we have made the most of our lives.

When I think about the thirty years Mrs W has spent in writing essays, I am reminded of our own way of life. It does not lead to any particular destination. It is not meant to conquer any summit. We spend most of our time with an essay as our companion. When we publish what we have written in the form of a book, we are able to send our messages out into the world, and experience the pleasure of having accomplished something thus far in the journey of life. If we are able to make the journey with friends who can offer words of encouragement along the way, the pleasure of travelling is sure to increase. If our friends actually also enjoy essay-writing themselves, the happier we will be.

List of Contributors

****

AYAKO AKUTSU
Born in 1935, I specialized in public health care study. I taught at a junior college, but retired many years ago. I am now enjoying life doing what I want to do. My two children left home a long time ago. I live with my husband. Japanese women enjoy the greatest longevity in the world. Both my mother and my husband's mother are one hundred years old. It is a pleasure listening to both of them talking about their amazing experiences when they were young. I would like to let my children and grandchildren know about such stories by writing essays based on what I have heard from these old ladies.

KYOKO AMANO
I was born in 1948. I married soon after graduating junior college. Because my husband was regularly transferred to various parts of the country, I continued to live away from Tokyo. While living in Osaka, I contributed articles to a particular newspaper as a reporter. This experience stimulated my interest in writing essays by picking up themes from trivial events in everyday life. Now I live a tranquil life with my husband, who has retired from work. I love going off on my own for a casual trip somewhere. I am looking forward to realizing my dream of travelling alone to England one day.

CHIZUKO BANDO
I was born in 1943, and grew up in Tokyo. I graduated from Waseda University in 1966, majoring in Japanese Literature. I'm not very young, but not so old either. I now spend every day thinking, 'Today is the healthiest day of my life, today is the happiest day of my life

and today is the richest day of my life.' So, I'd like to live believing, 'TODAY IS THE BEST DAY.'

KEIKO BANDO
I was born in a town at the foot of Mt Fuji in 1963. At present I live with my husband and two sons – fifteen and eleven years old. Our home is located at Ryogoku in Tokyo, which is famous as the home of Sumo wrestling, Japan's national sport.

I work at a law office. I am fond of reading books and every year I borrow more than a hundred books from the library nearby. But the time I spend with my family is more important to me than my work at the office and reading books. I feel happiest when I stay at home during the holidays, enjoying our comfortable family life together.

KAZUKO F. FUJINO
Born in Tokyo in 1941, I graduated from the University of Tokyo in 1964. I was being trained to become a mental health counsellor at Mitsubishi Bank's head office, when in 1967 I married my husband who was a gastroenterologist. My hobbies include tea ceremony, calligraphy and gardening.

I gave birth to a child almost every year and have two daughters and two sons. I had to stay at home to take care of my children. At that time I began to write about our life in those days – now forty years ago. Since my children grew up, I have taught Japanese language and tea ceremony to overseas visitors and beginners.

When I lived in Yamanashi Province, I received awards for some of my essays. In translating my essays into English this time, my husband helped me a great deal despite being so busy; I thank him from the bottom of my heart for his support.

AIKO HAMADA
I was born in Kagoshima, the prefecture on the southern tip of Kyushu, in September 1937. After graduation, I married my husband, who was senior to me by one year at the same university. I lived a happy comfortable life with my affectionate husband and two sweet

daughters until my husband suddenly died of a subarachnoid hermorrhage in July 1989, at the age of fifty-two. Sunk in grief, I cried endlessly. It is entirely thanks to my daughters and many friends that I have recovered my peaceful everyday life. I should like to dedicate this book to my deceased husband, who used to teach at a senior high school. I am really grateful that I am a member of the writers' group.

MIKI HAMANE
I was born in Nagoya in 1950. I majored in Spanish at the university. Working as an interpreter of Spanish, I have visited about fifty countries, including England of course. I began writing essays when I was forty-one years old. I decided to do this because I wanted to find space for myself in the busy days of working and raising my son and daughter who are already independent. In 2007, my husband retired from his own company at the age of fifty-six. He loves chess and he wants to participate in the chess tournaments held in many cities around the world. I love writing and teaching essay writing. The second stage of our life has just begun.

FUMI ISHII
I was born in 1935. I live by myself because my family are already living their own lives. Now half my heart is occupied by essay-writing and half is occupied by my two sons, one daughter and four grandchildren. Thanks to my teacher, Professor Harumi Kimura, I am in charge of three essay classes. How I express my heart and my life in the essay gives me great happiness. About five years ago I had a delightful experience in The Chase in London. I would be very glad if you read the story about my little journey to the Soseki Museum in The Chase.

HITOMI ISHIWATARI
I have been writing essays for more than twenty years. I have three children. My eldest child is a boy who has autism. Each day is extremely busy. I get through it by taking time out to write my essays. It has now become an indispensable part of my life.

Three years ago a book of essays about our autistic son was published. The book felt like a fourth child for me but it has ventured out into the world and is standing on its own before any of the children. It fascinates me to see it do so well.

TOSHIO IWAKI
I was born in Hyogo prefecture in 1931. I graduated from the University of Kyoto in 1956. A Master of Science, I specialized in nuclear physics. Thereafter, I worked at Mitsubishi Atomic Power Industries, Inc. in the research and development of nuclear power plants such as PWR, FBR and HTGR for about thirty years.

In 1959, I was transferred to Brookhaven National Laboratory in the US for about one year in order to study experiments in reactor physics. From 1990 to 2000, I participated in the projects for the prevention of human error in operating nuclear power plants in collaboration with Human Reliability Associates Ltd, UK. I finally retired from Mitsubishi in 2001. In 2002, I began essay writing at the Harumi Kimura class of the Asahi Culture Centre in Tokyo. Today, I live alone after the death of my wife in 1999.

YASUKO IWASAKI
I was born in September 1928, and graduated from Atomi Women's Academy in Tokyo in 1945. I am a housewife. I published a book entitled *The Encounter with Good Things* in 1995, and published its second edition in 2005. I have had a particular liking for tea ceremony since I was a child. My hobby is to appreciate ceramic ware, Buddhist images, *Noh* plays, music and architecture. I love Japanese culture and take pride in it.

AKIKO IWASHITA
I have a daughter who is twenty-nine years old. She is very cheerful, optimistic and vivacious. She is kind to everybody, especially to my husband and me. Now she works hard as an engineer in environment technology. She is too busy to meet her companion for life by chance. So, I hope that she will marry as soon as possible and live a peaceful life.

JUNKO KAWAMURA
I was born in 1926. My favourite things are reading books, writing essays and visiting antique markets. As I get older, I seem to be less sensitive and often look back on my past. I hope there will be many encounters involving joy and pleasure in the limited time left of my life and I would write about them vividly in my essays.

KEIICHI KAWASAKI
I was born in Kumamoto in central Kyushu in 1929. In 1950, after finishing school, I began working at the Dai-ichi Bank (now Mizuho Bank). On retiring from the bank under the age limit in 1994, I started to study essay writing. My two children now live independently with my five grandchildren, and I live alone with my wife in Kamakura, one of the oldest cities in Japan. When I look back on my forty-year life at the bank, I find it was constantly concerned with money. At present I enjoy breathing the air of the old city, which still retains the atmosphere of the old Buddhist and samurai society of Japan's Middle Ages.

HARUMI KIMURA
Professor Emeritus of Kyoritsu Women's University. She graduated from the postgraduate school of Tokyo University of Education with a Master of Arts (English and American Literature) and has published many academic essays in English and Japanese. She stayed in London from 1974 to 1975 and her first book *Letters from London At Twilight* was awarded the eighth Ohya Soichi Nonfiction Award. Since then she has been active as a writer and a journalist in various fields. From 1984 to 1987 she was Chairwoman of the Subcommittee of the National Council on Educational Reform, under the Ministry of Prime Minister Yasuhiro Nakasone, in charge of lifelong learning. She is also teaching adult education clases in how to write essays. She is the president of KEG (Kimura Harumi Essayists' Group), which has published many books of Essays.

YOKO KISHITA
Born in 1928, I have lived here and there as I followed my husband's work. But, now I am settled here, near lake Teganuma – with my

husband and a cat, named Futaro. I'm going to write about my daily life.

SABURO KURAMOCHI
In this essay I want to emphasize the importance of minor characters in Shakespeare's dramas. A lot of critics often focus on the central characters, such as Hamlet, Othello, King Lear and Macbeth. It is true those characters impress us with their complex human nature and deep psychology, but some minor characters are important as well. Just as in haiku poetry small and humble things are often represented as beautiful, so in Shakespearian dramas marginal characters are meaningful and deserve our attention. They tell us that there are still serious problems to consider and solve.

KUNIO MACHIDA
I was born in Tokyo in 1930 and lived in China for eight years from 1938 to 1946, and then returned to Tokyo in 1946. After studying economics at university, I entered NTT (Nippon Telegraph and Telephone Co.) in 1953. I was engaged in the telecommunication business for forty-six years.

Soon after I retired, I joined an essay-writing class as a hobby.

I live alone with my wife. My daughter and son live apart from us.

However, occasionally they visit us with their children. I always look forward to their visits.

YASUKO MATSUMOTO
I graduated in Economics from Keio University, and worked in the accounting division of a general trading company for four years. After marriage, and while raising my children, I became interested in writing down events from everyday life.

Twelve years ago, I met Professor Harumi Kimura, who ran an essay-writing group (KEG), and that was when I began writing essays. I have written mainly about my family. My sons, my mother, my sisters, and sometimes my husband, appeared in my essays.

When I read my old essays, I feel as though I am opening the family album. They remind me of the memories of my sons' school days, birthdays, New Year's Day, Christmas's and other past events. Happiness and smiles live there. My family is talking to me. Those essays are my treasures forever.

SACHIKO MIBU
I was born in Tokyo in 1953. I spent my school years from primary school through to the end of high school at the Sacred Heart School in Tokyo and then went on to the University of the Sacred Heart also in Tokyo. I was married in 1977 and we have two sons. In 1980, my husband was transferred to London and we lived there for four years. Fifteen years have passed since I began writing essays about my family and daily life. Now, I am a lecturer in essay writing at the NHK Academy of Distance Learning. These days, I spend a lot of time correcting other people's essays so I feel I need to write more essays of my own. At the same time, I really enjoy reading essays of ordinary people such as those in this book.

KUMIKO MIURA
I was born in 1952. I graduated from Aichi Educational College, then I worked as a elementary school teacher, and I married in 1977. I have a daughter and two sons. I like playing tennis and enjoy playing with my husband a few times a week, and also taking part in local tournaments.

KIYOKO NAKAJIMA
I was born in Tokyo in 1939 and raised in the old capital of Kyoto. In my early years I contributed short articles to newspapers and magazines throughout Japan, and in the past twenty years I have been devoting my time to writing essays. I enjoy writing about everyday events familiar to the Japanese but also, because of my family's long history on the stage, my essays are often about the performing arts. My husband and son, following the family tradition, are professional performers of Japanese *nagauta.* I also sing *nagauta* as a hobby. Recently I have been performing chanson and canzone on the stage as a semi-professional.

KAYOKO NAKAMURA
I was born in Tokyo in 1955. After graduating from Sophia University in Tokyo, I taught at a primary school for three years. I am fond of travelling and gardening. Ten years ago, my husband was transferred to Alberta State, Canada, and I accompanied him with my two children, who were in primary school and junior high school respectively. I enjoyed my life there for a year, surrounded by nature. I was helped a lot by my friend from Britain, to whom I am looking forward to sending this book.

SEIKO NAKAMURA
I was born in 1944. After graduating from Chiba University, which was located not so far from my house, I taught at a primary school in Tokyo. Later, I worked as a librarian at a primary school in Chiba Prefecture, and coached students in reading classes. The city where I worked put a great deal of effort into developing reading at all levels and a large number of people from all parts of Japan visited to see what was being done. I often introduced books or read them to the pupils.

I am fond of travelling. I should like to go over to England some day and visit Shakespeare's birthplace, the scene of Wuthering Heights and Peter Rabbit's home town.

YUKIKO NISHIDA
I was born in February 1945, in the city of Kanazawa on the coast of the Sea of Japan, one of the snowy districts. According to Japanese custom, my mother gave birth to me at her parents' home. Receiving the news of the birth of his new daughter, in Tokyo, my father hurried to Kanazawa on the train pulled by a steam locomotive. All day long, it snowed heavily. So, he decided to name his new baby Yukiko. 'Yuki' means snow in Japanese.

YOSHIKO OBATA
My favourite flower is the marguerite. When I look at something living, I love the space extending to it. In arranging flowers, for example, I think of ways of making full use of the beauty of each flower.

The same thing can be said of writing essays. Five years ago, I moved from Kyoto to Tokyo – from the old capital to the present one. In writing an essay, I always find myself changing what I have written. When a day is over, I discover another mother living within me.

AKIKO OHNO
Born in Tokyo in 1940, I graduated in English and American literature at a college in Tokyo, and also studied English teaching method at a university in America. After my marriage, I lived in Germany and Holland for ten years. During that time, I learned German and Dutch, and did my best to understand their culture. I also visited various countries in Europe with my family. Since returning to Tokyo, I have been trying to introduce Japanese culture to foreigners living in Japan.

KEIKO OHTAKE
I have been learning Japanese calligraphy. The text we use is a book entitled *Shoho-Genzo*, written in Japanese by Dogen (1200-53), a Zen Buddhist priest of the Kamakura Period (1183–1333), on the essence of Buddhism. 'To live is as ephemeral as to die', a phrase from the book, sounds enchanting and contains profound meaning. I write Japanese characters on Japanese paper with a Japanese brush, chanting and tasting the text.

KATSUKO OKA
I was born in Hiroshima in 1932. I married soon after graduating from Tokyo Woman's Christian College. My first book, entitled 'The Philosophy of A Common Woman' is about daily life in my fifties. The next one is how to get along with my husband's disease for ten years. Since my husband died I have been living alone. Writing essays has become my routine, as well as watching, listening, talking, travelling and thinking.

KYOKO OKUDA
I am a housewife in my late fifties. My hobby is travelling and playing the *koto*, the Japanese harp. I have been to Kyoto in kimono and hope to travel abroad in kimono some day. My husband will soon

reach the retirement age limit at his work. None of my three children is married. My pets – a sixteen-year-old dog and four cats – help to make my home a very lively place.

Recently I have come to enjoy writing essays. I should like to go on writing, looking back on my past and rediscovering good Japanese characteristics.

ASAKO ONO
I was born in Tokyo in 1959. After I graduated at St Paul's University in Tokyo, I worked at Hitachi High-Technologies Corporation, and retired from work when I married. Motivated by curiosity, I have been writing essays for more than a decade. My father, who I refer to in my essay, is ill in bed with cancer and will not live to see this book published. I have been told that we can fulfil ourselves only when we have got over the grief of losing our parents, but I am not sure I can do that. Still, I should like to continue writing essays on aspects of everyday life until the day when I cannot write any more, believing that both joys and sorrows are presents from God.

HATSUKO SAKAMOTO
I was born in 1931. When I was young, I worked at the lower court as a typist. But I made up my mind to become a beauty specialist, and moved to Tokyo. Since then, it has been my work for fifty years. Meanwhile, my husband died thirteen years ago. Now, I sometimes think about retirement.

MICHIYO SASAKI
I have been a housewife for forty-two years since I married after graduating from Rikkyo University. I have two daughters, but I now live alone with my husband who used to be a government official.

I enjoy writing essays because it helps me understand my inner self that cannot be reflected in a mirror. I like travel, growing flowers and appreciating works of art.

MIDORI SEKIGUCHI
Five years ago, I stayed at a B&B in the Perthshire countryside with my daughter, who was then a college student. A widow aged sixty

looked after the flowers, dogs and hens there on her own. I thought that her independent life surrounded by her favourite things was an ideal life. She seemed to be busy in the evening. So we volunteered to take her dogs for a walk. By the roadside, I found some thistles similar to those in my garden. Anybody can live anywhere. I wondered if I should ask her to stay with us to take care of the flowers and animals for a while. Such a fantastic idea made my heart fill with joy.

ATSUKO SHIMAKAWA

I was born in Tokyo in 1935. I was brought up by my grandparents in a small village in Ehime Prefecture in Shikoku from the age of five until I was eighteen.

After finishing high school, I went up to Tokyo and lived by and for myself, studying at a dressmaking school. I worked hard for nearly ten years and then got married.

At the age of fifty-eight, I began to write essays to prevent my mind from growing old. Now it makes me feel my life is worth living. I am a housewife. I have two sons, one of whom lives with my husband and me.

KEIKO TAKANO

I was born in January 1938. I married after graduating at Jissen Women's University in Tokyo. I find myself hardly changed in mind though I am much advanced in age. At present I continue to study while teaching in the essay-writing class at the culture centre.

My husband, who has retired from work, and I have lived with our eldest son and his family for ten years. Now my three grandchildren have grown up and we have been enjoying a comfortable, peaceful life.

SETSUKO TERAO

Almost forty years have passed since I lived in Germany with my husband and two pre-school-age boys. It was a time when still very few Japanese went abroad. As everything we saw and heard was full of wonder, so were we ourselves new to the European people. After we came back home I joined the essay class to write about what we experienced there. Although we have been to Europe several times since,

'B&B in Sweden' remains one of the best recollections of our family trip to northern Europe while we were staying in Germany.

YUKI TEZUKA
About ten years ago, I joined the essay class. A few years later, a baby girl was born. She was so cute and laughed a lot. I often wrote about her.

We visited many places, of course. We visited London, my favourite city, when she was one year old. What sweet and lovely days they were! Then three years later, we had twin boys!! It was like a battlefield in our house – screaming in the bedroom, something crashing in the living-room. Of course, there was no time to write an essay. I almost gave up writing. But this year, they are old enough to go to kindergarten, so I decided to write again. I hope this will be a turning point in my life.

MAYUMI TOMIYAMA
I was born in Hiroshima in 1944. I live alone with my husband in Tokyo after my son and daughter got married several years ago.

About ten years ago, I began ballroom dancing with my husband. Dancing to the rhythm and good sweating rejuvenated my mind and body. It is a good supplement for me. Some day I wish to dance at the famous Blackpool dancing competition in England. That is my dream.

MIKIKO TSUNODA
A widow, born in 1926, I experienced the Second World War in my youth. When I was twenty-one I married in Tokyo much of which still consisted of burnt ruins after the war. As a typical devoted housewife for over fifty-three years, I have been blessed with two sons, four granddaughters and five great-grandchildren. I'm very good at making dresses, and my hobbies are mountaineering, writing essays, photography and cooking. I have enjoyed mountain-climbing in Nepal, China and Pakistan as well as in Japan. The highest peak I ever reached is 5,416 metres high. My book, *I Shall Never Forget Mountains and You*, was published in 2002. I am now eighty-two, still walking around mountain paths with wonderful friends – my treasures.

MITSUO URATA

I was born in Tokyo in 1932, and was employed by the Tokyo Metropolitan Government. I married in 1962 and lost my better half in 1999. I have been teaching Japanese to foreigners for sixteen years and also teaching essay writing. I like to climb mountains (the highest mountain I have ever climbed is Kilimanjaro in Africa), to listen to rakugo and classic music, to appreciate operas, operettas and pictures, to watch sumo wrestling, to travel abroad. I am now living in Tokyo with the children.

SAKI USHIDO

When I get tired by the rigours of the day, I envy the tropical fish which swim in a coral reef. I can see that the tropical fish do not worry about anything, but merely flutter about gracefully in the water. But if I were a fish, I might find every day very tedious.

I am a housewife. My family consists of four people – me, my husband, our daughter and our son. Our daughter and the son are not yet married. They are in their thirties.

I used to love volleyball, calligraphy and making cakes. Now, I sometimes write an essay and I live a leisurely life.

YOKO USUDA

I was born in 1957. One of my hobbies is walking with my husband. I began writing essays to record the happy events of my family. It is very hard to create, but finishing an essay brings me a feeling of satisfaction. I hope that I continue to write from hereon.

HIROKO YAMADA

I was born in Kyoto in 1944. I have been married for almost forty years. My husband was a businessman. My two sons, who are also businessmen, are married and live with their own families. I have three grandchildren.

Kyoto is an old city with a 1,200-year-old history. Japanese tea ceremony parties are often held at the shrines and temples in the city. I sometimes enjoy participating in those parties, wearing Japanese kimono.

KAORI YAMAMOTO
I was born in Tokyo, and finished a course in business studies at Los Angeles City College in 1976. I taught English at elementary school and often encouraged pupils not to hesitate to speak English. English is the most effective tool of communication so far for foreign people. I like to travel, and to visit old cities and interesting countries. Two sons have started working already. The older is an architect in the making, the younger is a systems engineer, and my husband is also an engineer and likes to paint in watercolours. Our common hobby is music. Rocky the old dog, a Maltese, is always with me.

TAKAKO YASUGI
I have been studying essay writing for four years. When I was young, I was just a roving girl. When I was sixty-five, I decided I would like to start writing essays about the old days. I try to find essay schools using the internet and found the essay class of the Sankei School. When I realized that I had a poor vocabulary and little talent for writing, I reflected on my poor study performance in my youth.

YOKO YOSHIDA
I was born in 1941 and graduated from Waseda University in 1966, having majored in Japanese Literature. I married soon after graduation.

I have three children – one son and two daughters. Each of my three children has graduated from university, is employed and married. I live now with my husband who retired from his office ten years ago. I have six grandchildren.

YURIKO YOSHIHARA
I was born in Tokyo in 1953. At the age of ten, I spent two years in Beirut in Lebanon, at an international school where I became friends with a number of people from various countries and came to be interested in the different cultures of their countries. My strong consciousness of my being Japanese made me specialize in Japanese literature at Keio University. I am now teaching Japanese language and

literature at Atomi High School, a private school in Tokyo. In my class I always endeavour to encourage my students to recognize the beauty of the Japanese language in classical works. I should like to write essays, setting a high value on the characteristic sense of the Japanese.

List of Translators

****

ATSUKO BABA
Freelance translator. She has twenty years experience in English and Japanese translations, mainly consisting of patents, manuals for machinery and legal documents. She lived overseas for fifteen years in the four cities of Montreal (Canada), Oakland (California), Singapore and Jakarta (Indonesia).

PHILIP HALTMAN
Born in The United States and attended William Paterson University in the State of New Jersey, majoring in vocal performance. Upon moving to Tokyo, he began teaching English and learning Japanese. He is active in his own school, Sunmuse English, where he and Maiko, his wife, teach every day. They also take part in concerts and give volunteer performances in nursing homes throughout Tokyo and the nearby areas. Maiko helps Philip with his translations.

NAOMITSU KUMABE
Honorary Professor of Research for Language Teaching in Japan, successor to Harold E Palmer, who introduced the Oral Method to Japan in 1924. Major field: English Education. Main writer of the textbooks 'Everyday English' (Chukyou Shuppan) and 'Royal English' (Ohbunsha), authorized by the Ministry of Education.

Went over to the US as a Fulbright exchange teacher and was awarded an honorary citizenship of Texas in 1961.

SABURO KURAMOCHI
Professor emeritus of Tokyo University of Liberal Arts and Education.

Between 1994 and 1996, he was the president of Japan D.H. Lawrence Society.

Studied as an occasional student at the postgraduate school, Birkbeck College, University of London. Received his Ph.D. in literature at Tsukuba University.

He is the author of many academic publications and essays in English on D.H. Lawrence, Shakespeare and so on. He is also a poet and has published many books of poems.

HARUKO MIYAZAKI
Haruko Miyazaki is a lecturer of English at Rikkyo University and Tokyo University of Marine Science and Technology. She also works as a translator at TV Asahi. She is co-author of *How to Write Letters and Cards in English*, Shinsei Shuppan, 1998.

YURI TAKAHASHI
Professor of English in the Faculty of Policy Informatics at Chiba University of Commerce, and a Senior Instructor at the International Training Institute of NHK, the Japan Broadcasting Corporation, a public radio and television broadcaster in Tokyo, where the work involves planning, coordinating and teaching the training courses for aspiring interpreters and translators. She is co-author of *Wake Up Your Dormant English*, Hamano Shuppan, 2004, and *Introduction to English Interpretation*, Taishukan Shoten, 2007.

Acknowledgements

It is perhaps the first time that a group of Japanese individuals have had their essays published in the United Kingdom. It is only eight months ago since this ambitious publication was first planned, and we owe a great debt to a number of people for its realization. I would now like to acknowledge those people and offer them my sincere gratitude.

When I discussed my intention to publish the essays with Junji Doi, Director of the Tokyo Office of the Great Britain-Sasakawa Foundation, he at once made contact with Stephen McEnally, Director of the British Office, who introduced me to Paul Norbury at Global Oriental publishers. Without their support and agreement to publish our book in the United Kingdom our 'dream' would never have been realized.

It was Paul Norbury who proposed the title of this book. He clearly understood what our aims were in publishing our writings and gave it a clear and attractive title. My contact with him was entirely through e-mail and by phone, but there was no doubt we had found a good partner that we could rely on. I really appreciate his collaboration in bringing about publication of *Living Japan.*

The value of a book of translated writings partly depends on the availability of excellent translators. In this regard, I was reassured that it would be possible to find and work with such outstanding English translators. Those who agreed to work on the project are probably amongst the best qualified in Japan. Some of them are friends to the members of our group; others are my friends from my university days. They are introduced elsewhere in this book.

When I told my family, friends and acquaintances about my plan for publishing this book, they all recognized its uniqueness and gave their support, which greatly encouraged me.

Last but not least, I must thank the people of the 'Writer's Group Promoting Japanese Culture' (represented by Ms Yasuko Matsumoto), who, sharing the same interest with us, offered essays to KEG (Kimura-Harumi Essayist Group). Without their collaboration, the publication of this book would not have been possible. All of these contributors are very proud of the fact that their essays have been translated into English and will be read by a great number of English-speaking readers around the world. I should also like to acknowledge Mitsuo Urata who very kindly mediated between the writers and translators and Ms Yasuko Matsumoto who liaised with the publishing company regarding our formal agreement. I also wish to acknowledge Tosio Iwaki and his collaboration in finalizing all the texts and sending them to the publisher in Britain. All the authors introduce themselves elsewhere in this volume. They are my lifelong friends.

HARUMI KIMURA

Index

****